Praise for
Live Kind, Be Happy

Celeste and Louis seamlessly weave together science and page-turning stories of kindness, convincing us that kindness is a recipe for long-term happiness. This lovely book offers simple yet powerful practices to bring more kindness and happiness into your life and the lives of those around you. Read it yourself, then give copies to the people you care most about in this world.

—**Michelle McQuaid**, best-selling author and host of *Making Positive Psychology Work* podcast

With authenticity and a sound platform of research, Celeste gets to the heart of happiness: how we can use kindness to make our own lives better while improving the world around us. I love Celeste's writing style, and I know you will too. It feels like you're sitting with a wise and compassionate friend!

—**Nicole J. Phillips**, host of *The Kindness Podcast* and author of *The Negativity Remedy*

Live Kind, Be Happy is perfectly timed. Our fractured and stressed world has fostered rising anxiety, depression, unhappiness, and other mental health problems. According to global surveys by the World Health Organization, anxiety and depression are the two most prevalent emotional disorders in the world. We are in the middle of a mental health pandemic, and the whole world is desperate for a kinder, safer, and happier place to live.

Based on bona fide science, this book makes a convincing case for becoming happier through kindness. The authors provide concrete guidance in the form of simple practices that can be done organically in the course of daily life. The results may surprise and delight you.

Celeste DiMilla's writing style is authentic, skillful, and engaging, and she will keep you motivated to discover happiness by practicing simple acts of kindness. Her personal journey toward kindness is endearing, and readers are likely to identify with the challenge of developing new thinking patterns and behavior habits. This book will lead you on the path to kindness, which if enough people participate could transform the world into a happier place to live.

—**Paul Foxman, PhD,** founder and director of Vermont Center for Anxiety Care, Burlington, Vermont, and author of *Dancing with Fear* (2007), *The Worried Child* (2003), and *The Clinician's Guide to Anxiety Disorders in Kids and Teens* (2017)

Live Kind, Be Happy is a treasure trove of insights into the connection between kindness and happiness. A wonderfully inspirational read!

—**Orly Wahba**, founder and CEO of Life Vest Inside and author of *Kindness Boomerang*

There are so many books telling us what's wrong with us. There are very few telling us what's right about us. This book gives us hope and lets us know that even the smallest thing can change our own lives and the lives of those around us.

—**Brooke Jones**, vice president of The Random Acts of Kindness Foundation

It is my hope that reading this book opens up the tremendous and renewable energy source that is kindness. And I hope that from there we can start imagining and implementing kindness on a societal and structural level.

—**Kristen Truempy**, host of the *Positive Psychology Podcast*

If you seek long-term happiness and care deeply about making the world a better place, then put this book on your required reading list. You will learn tons of simple and practical kindness practices that will not only boost your own happiness and well-being but do the same for those you love and everyone around you.

—**Emiliya Zhivotovskaya**, CEO and founder of The Flourishing Center

Live Kind, Be Happy

Beth & George,
May you guys
always be
happy ☺
Celeste

Live Kind, Be Happy

How Simple Science-Based Kindness Practices Can Make You Happier

Celeste DiMilla, MS, LMFT, CAPP
with Louis Alloro, MEd, MAPP

OH HAPPY DAY PUBLISHING
Laguna Niguel, CA

Cover and book design: Asya Blue Design
LCCN: 2021911468
ISBN 978-1-7373279-0-5 (paperback)
ISBN 978-1-7373279-1-2 (e-book)

Printed in the United States of America

celestedimilla.com

To Ron and Lorrie Wenzler,
extraordinary role models of kindness.

CONTENTS

INTRODUCTION

How Practicing Kindness Transformed My Life and Made Me Happier

This book started in, of all places, a bathroom at the Los Angeles International Airport (don't worry, it was pretty clean). I was at the sink trying to find "the sweet spot" to get the water to flow, but no luck. The middle-aged woman at a neighboring sink smiled brightly at me, stepped back, and said, "Here, you can use mine."

"Thanks," I said, feeling appreciative. I moved over to take her place at the sink, and as she exited the restroom, I overheard her say to a woman waiting in the line for the stalls, "I just had to stop and tell you that you're beautiful."

My heart sank. She hadn't said anything to me about how I looked. Why not?

I sneaked a peek at the other woman—a tall, slender, fashionably dressed twentysomething brunette with amazing cheekbones. Then I looked at myself in the mirror. My softly layered golden-brown hair framed my face nicely. My skin was clear with a rosy glow, and there were no discernible wrinkles. I didn't think I looked bad for someone who was fifty. And that's when it hit.

Oh my God, I'm FIFTY!

The reality of my advancing age hit me like a ton of bricks, even though I'd already been fifty for several months. My life, unless I was exceptionally fortunate, *was more than half over.* What on earth had I done with the past half century?

I left the bathroom with my brain in negative overdrive, and by the time my husband Paul and I boarded our flight to Boston to visit his family, I'd convinced myself that I'd done nothing of significance with my life. I was an underachiever, a loser, a big fat zero. As I slumped into my seat, I thought, *Uh-oh, I'm having a midlife crisis.*

As I watched my husband wipe off his armrest, I thought about how I'd likely been in the midst of a midlife crisis before this moment but hadn't realized it. I'd actually been feeling like my life lacked meaning for the past few years. I didn't have children to give me a sense of purpose, and my vision of changing people's lives through my career as a psychotherapist hadn't panned out like I thought it would. In fact, I wasn't even *working* as said psychotherapist!

Here's exactly how that happened: After getting my marriage and family therapist (MFT) license, I opened a psychotherapy practice with much anticipation of helping people. Then I spent months waiting for someone to call (not exaggerating!). Two years into my practice I was still floundering, with only three clients. So when Paul and I had to relocate for his work, I actually felt relieved that I had to close my practice. I figured that moving would give me the chance to start a fresh psychotherapy practice, but after Paul and I settled into our new home I procrastinated. I was scared: What if I failed again? What if I couldn't really help people? What if I never did anything meaningful with my life?

In an attempt to motivate myself and find some inspiration over the past year, I started reading self-help books. The one I was currently reading, *Creating Your Best Life* by Caroline Adams Miller and Michael Frisch, was in my carry-on bag.[1] Wanting to get my mind off my troubled thoughts, I pulled out the book and started reading. I read somewhat distractedly at first, but then on page eight I read: "we are living longer and healthier lives, which has changed the midlife crisis into the midlife opportunity."

Opportunity . . . hunh. It felt like the authors were speaking directly to me. I dog-eared the page, put a star by the sentence, and wrote *midlife opportunity* in bold lettering in the margin.

I continued reading, now at a feverish pace. And read I did—during the entire flight, in the car on the way to our hotel, sitting in the bathroom late that night (I didn't want any lights on in our room to keep my husband awake), while in a coffee shop the next morning, and then in the coin shop where my husband was selling his late father's collection.

I finished the book in two days. I also completed many of the exercises in the book, most of which involved creating a list of life goals. As I reviewed my list, I noticed that the first goal I'd written was *prioritize kindness*.

This was telling. Kindness had always been one of my deepest values, but I had to admit that I didn't always live as if it were. My life just seemed to be too busy to do the kind things I wanted to do, like train my wonderful fluffy white dog, Mambo, to be a therapy dog or teach free Laughter Yoga classes at our local senior center.

While having dinner that night with my husband and mother-in-law, I was troubled by the thought that I wasn't as kind as I truly wanted to be. I mulled this over while sipping a strong mai tai and came to the conclusion that my midlife opportunity was . . . *kindness!*

I felt a true sense of urgency about this: I had to do something really big *right now* to make up for lost time—a *half century* of lost time. My tipsy brain immediately formulated a plan, and in the midst of our quiet dinner I burst out, "I'm going to do something outrageously kind every day from now on!"

My mother-in-law looked at my husband and, with raised eyebrows, asked, "Is she for real?"

Used to my excitable nature, Paul didn't even look up from his pad thai noodles while matter-of-factly responding, "Yep, that's my wife."

Despite receiving very little fanfare upon uttering my for-a-lifetime promise, I was serious and undeterred. On the drive back to our hotel, I contemplated what I could do to be outrageously kind the very next day.

Maybe I can serve food at a soup kitchen over the next few days. No, that will take too much time away from visiting with family whom I only get to see twice a year. Hmm . . . what else could I do while I'm up here in Boston visiting family?

After a bit I decided to begin my daily practice of what I had deemed "outrageous kindness" by doing a lot of small kindnesses, like giving large tips and paying for the coffee of the person behind me. I rationalized that I could fit these in whenever I had a spare moment, and if I did enough of them—perhaps dozens a day?—this could be considered "outrageously kind."

The next day I woke up determined to follow through with being outrageously kind. The first thing I did was to write a thank-you note for the housekeeper—and leave next to it a very large tip. When Paul noticed this, however, he said, "I want you to know that I support you in whatever it is you're doing, but I'd appreciate it if you could find ways to be kind without spending a lot of money."

My heart sank at his words, and I must admit, I pouted for a while. After I thought about it, however, I knew he was right. We didn't have the resources for me to give money away dozens of times a day. So I caved and responded, "Okay." It was obvious a different strategy was needed to fulfill my goal of being outrageously kind.

So while Paul drove us to a local coffee shop a little while later, I began texting several friends and family members to tell them how wonderful I thought they were and how much I appreciated them. I was bummed when no one immediately replied, but then I remembered that the people I'd sent messages to were all in California—and it wasn't even 5:00 a.m. there yet!

Once we arrived at the coffee shop, I sat at a table while Paul waited at the counter for our lattes. There was an elderly couple sitting quietly at the table next to me, so I scribbled *May you be happy* on a napkin and handed it to them. They perked up, smiled at me, and said, "Thank you!" with so much feeling that I could tell they really appreciated my attention. Wow! Being kind felt wonderful.

While considering what other kindnesses I could do that day, I received a gushing, emoji-filled text message from my early riser of a mom telling me "how nice" it was to wake up to the text I'd sent. I felt like I'd really made her day, and this too warmed my heart.

When I looked up from the phone, my husband handed me our drinks and left to use the bathroom. While he was away, I wrote a silly love poem to him on his paper coffee cup. When he returned and noticed it, he smiled broadly and said, "You're a nut, and that's why I love you so much!"

I was grinning as I too left to use the bathroom, which was down a hallway past several businesses. On my way back to the coffee shop I peered into a gym through a big glass window, and the young woman working there smiled at me. I decided that for my next kindness, I'd thank her. So I walked into the gym and said, "Thank you for smiling at me. I really appreciate that. You know, it's just so nice when people smile."

She seemed taken aback, but in a delighted way. Then, without even thinking about it, I said, "I'm doing this kindness thing, and I feel like giving you a hug. Are you okay with that?"

She seemed moved by this and we embraced. I felt so happy after this that I bounded down the hallway back to the coffee shop and excitedly told Paul what I had done. He didn't lift his head up from his phone as he brushed me off with a "That's nice, sweetie." But I didn't mind because my string of small kindnesses had boosted my mood considerably.

I continued doing kindnesses like this for the rest of that day and managed to get in a whopping forty-eight. For the next five days of our vacation I kept on with this practice, and by the time we boarded our flight home, I felt happier than I had in years. The past week had literally transformed me; I felt excited about life again!

⌒

Paul and I arrived home from our trip to Boston on a Monday, and I was fully committed to practicing outrageous kindness that Tuesday. But I woke up late and as I thought about my long after-vacation to-do list, doing dozens of kind acts felt like too much of a burden on my already busy day. I rationalized that once I caught up with my chores, I'd go back to being outrageously kind.

Wednesday came with its usual stressors, so I put off my kindness priority again. And when I failed to practice it for the rest of the week, I vowed to start fresh on Monday. It didn't happen, and when another two weeks passed without performing a daily regimen of dozens of kindnesses, I began to wonder if I'd ever succeed. I was blowing my midlife opportunity, and this recognition bummed me out.

The fear of blowing it motivated me for a while, and I pushed myself to be outrageously kind. It worked for a few days here and there. Like the day I talked Paul and my sister, Michelle, into spending an afternoon with me brightly painting smooth small rocks with positive messages like "Spread love" and "Choose joy" and then leaving them in various places around Imperial Beach, California, for people to discover. While such days boosted my mood and made me want to do more, I found it difficult to be outrageously kind on a regular basis. Somehow it just seemed . . . too hard.

Then one day while washing the dishes, I listened to an episode on *The One You Feed* podcast titled "The #1 Mistake People Make When Trying to Change Behavior."[2] Host Eric Zimmer said the mistake people make is "starting too big." He gave the example of how when he first started meditating, he tried to sit for thirty minutes a day. This was so hard for him, however, that he'd manage for only a day or two and then quit. This happened over and over until he decided to start small and meditate for just two minutes a day. Over time he gradually built up his new practice to thirty minutes daily. Starting small made all the difference for him.

Hearing Eric's story reminded me that I had a strikingly

similar experience with my own meditation practice—but also that starting small was how I managed to develop a daily exercise habit *and* transition to a plant-based diet. It dawned on me that I was making the number one behavior-change mistake in trying to go from "normal" kindness to "outrageous" kindness overnight! It was like going from couch potato to marathon runner overnight, which is, well, outrageous. ☺

If I truly wanted to become a kinder person and maintain this for the rest of my life, the key was to start small.

I immediately let go of trying to be outrageously kind and developed a small-steps approach. I began by making a list of kindness practices I wanted to do more of. On it were things like:

- Being more generous
- Speaking more kindly to myself
- Creating micro-moments of love (more on this in chapter 6)
- Doing random acts of kindness
- Being kind to unkind people

I derived the items on this list from my mindfulness practice and psychology—especially positive psychology, the scientific study of what makes life worth living. Once the list was complete, I decided to focus on doing just one practice per week.

Right away I noticed several positive things with my new small-steps approach. The first one was that I actually did my weekly practice. (Round of applause!) I'm not saying I always followed through, but I was much more consistent than I had been when I was trying to practice outrageous kindness. I also noticed that I got more pleasure from practicing—likely because I didn't feel stressed about squeezing lots of kind acts into my hectic daily schedule. And what surprised me most is that even such a small increase in my kindness lifted my spirits and made me feel happier.

Over time I noticed additional benefits, such as relationships with important people in my life improving. I simply felt closer and more connected to these significant people when I was being kinder to them. I also got the sense that those I cared for felt closer to me as well. In fact, all these people were also, well, being kinder to me as well. My husband, for example, started writing me little notes to make me smile—and began cleaning the kitchen more often!

Another benefit I noticed was that I felt less anxious and less overwhelmed. I thought this was strange at first, but I later learned that research suggests kindness buffers the negative effects of stress. Being kind puts your focus on *others*—which distracts you from your own worries and issues.

I also felt like I had truly embraced my midlife opportunity and was living in accord with my deepest values. Being a little kinder mattered! It made a difference in my life and in the lives of those around me, and it made a difference in the world. (Kindness ripples out! I promise, there'll be more on this later.)

And happily, the more I practiced, the more kindness became my default mode in life. What a wonderful discovery that was!

Goodness knows, I'm still far from Mother Teresa–like goodness, but I'm improving.

Doing one simple kindness practice per week has been life-changing; in fact, it affected me so much that I thought, *Maybe I'll write a book on this so others can benefit too!* The problem was that I was already cowriting another book with Louis Alloro, my instructor from my certification in applied positive psychology program (CAPP), a wonderful six-month personal and professional training program I'd just completed. He and I were writing a positive psychology manual for therapists and other professionals.

While I believed this manual was worthwhile, it also felt like an overwhelming undertaking for two novice writers. Plus, now I was on fire for kindness—that's what my heart truly wanted to write about. I felt torn: *Should I continue working on the manual or switch to writing a book about kindness?*

I shared my dilemma with Louis, and he kindly told me to follow my heart—that he'd support me with whatever I decided to do. We decided to continue to collaborate but transition to writing a book on kindness and happiness. Our plan was to share my personal experiences in the work, while together we'd present what science is discovering about the connection between kindness and happiness. Thus, the information and exercises in this book are a collaborative effort between Louis and me—although when the text says "I," it will be referring to a personal belief, experience, or insight of mine (Celeste).

The book is intended to help you understand the connection between kindness and happiness. More than that, it is intended to help you become a little kinder and a lot happier—something that will also ripple out and create a kinder and happier world.

However, merely reading this book is unlikely to make that happen. To have a real impact on your life and the lives of those around you, you have to *do* the kindness practices. That's right, there's actual work involved!

But don't panic: this will be simple if you take it one small step at a time (as I learned, and as you'll learn how to do in this book).

Here's how Louis and I are going to offer what we know now about kindness and the science of it to you.

In part 1, you will learn about the connection between kindness and happiness, because it's stronger than you think. In these chapters you'll start by taking a fresh look at kindness, which is helpful because you probably haven't formally studied this topic since you were in kindergarten (and if you're anything like Louis and me, that feels like a long time ago). Next, you'll learn why being kind makes *you* (not just others) happy. After this, you'll discover the benefits of kindness—the happiness of others, yourself, and the world being chief among them. You'll wrap it up with just why you are going to succeed at being a kinder person to yourself, others, and the world.

Then, in part 2, you'll learn a variety of simple, evidence-based ways to practice kindness in your daily life. These kindness practices are "seeds"—seeds to plant and grow kindness and happiness in the many aspects of your life; seeds you can watch as they blossom and bear fruit each day. And seeds aren't scary at all—in fact, they're quite small and easy to handle, aren't they?

Louis and I are delighted to share these life-changing, and we believe *world*-changing, kindness practices with you. By doing these simple practices, you can be the change—yes, *you!*

You can be:

- The change in yourself
- The change in those you care about
- The change in the world

How's that for taking a midlife opportunity and turning it into not only a personal opportunity, but a worldwide opportunity?

XO
Celeste (and Louis too!)

PART 1

The Connection between Kindness and Happiness

CHAPTER 1

A Fresh Look at Kindness

Kindness is more than deeds.
It is an attitude, an expression, a look, a touch.
It is anything that lifts another person.

—C. Neil Strait

So what *is* kindness, anyway? If Louis and I are writing a book about it, all of us—that means Louis and I, as well as you, our reader—had better be on the same page about it! It's common to think of kindness as a positive action that lifts someone up, and it *is* this. To clarify further: Kind actions don't have to be extravagant, such as giving your second car to someone who needs it more than you do, or spending hours and hours volunteering. A kind positive action that lifts up the party on the receiving end might be as simple as:

- Patiently listening to a friend who's struggling
- Helping a neighbor pack for a move
- Treating a coworker to lunch

- Reading a book to a child
- Giving someone the benefit of the doubt
- Comforting yourself when you make a mistake or fail (yes, that's right, it's important to be kind to yourself too!)

Kindness can also be about acts you refrain from doing. Not joining in on "trash talk" about someone, resisting the urge to get even, not judging others, refraining from yelling at your child or partner because they did something annoying, not giving someone attitude just because you're in a bad mood, or stopping yourself from giving unsolicited advice are all ways to be kind. An example from my own life—which reveals what it's like to *not* extend kindness during a friendly interaction— occurred while I was chatting with an older gentleman at a park while our dogs were playing together. This man corrected my grammar at one point, embarrassing me. It would have been much kinder of him to simply leave this comment unsaid.

Kindness is more than deeds; however, it's also an attitude or way of approaching life. Holding an attitude of kindness means embracing the belief that being kind and compassion- ate to everyone, *always*, is the best way to live. The Dalai Lama expressed this belief when he said, "Be kind whenever possible; it is always possible."

Holding an attitude of kindness doesn't mean you always act on this belief but that it is a way of life you value. As I learned from my own midlife crisis, sometimes we don't always live in accordance with our values. That's why it's important to note that we all can strengthen our attitude of kindness. (That's what this book will help you do.) Attitude is like a muscle, and if you exercise it, it gets stronger. Just as someone can work on strengthening a positive attitude, you can work on strengthening an attitude of kindness.

Even tiny acts of kindness—a kind word, listing to someone, or even a smile—can have a big impact on others and on your own state of mind. Mark, for example, says he will never forget how appreciative he was when a passenger offered to change seats with his wife so he could sit next to her on the flight he'd booked to Ohio last minute after his father died. It was a small courtesy, but it really mattered to Mark, making one of the most difficult days of his life a little easier and a little better.

In her book *A Short Course in Kindness*, Margot Silk Forrest says:

> *"One of the amazing things about kindness is how little it takes to make us feel great, whether we are on the receiving end or the giving end."*[3]

Let's take a moment to dispel some common misconceptions about kindness. Here are four things that kindness is *not*.

#1: Kindness is not about being a doormat.

When I was in high school, my friend Diana told me, "You're too nice." She didn't mean that I was too kind; rather she meant that I was a doormat—that I bent over backward for others while neglecting my own needs. It took me a long time to realize that being a doormat isn't kind. Kindness is about recognizing that all people, including yourself, are worthy of compassion, tenderness, and care. As meditation teacher Sharon Salzberg says:

> *"You yourself, as much as anybody in the entire universe, deserve your love and affection."*[4]

Besides, if you end up sacrificing your needs for others, you end up resentful, depleted, and unable to be kind to anyone.

Buddhist teacher Pema Chodron puts it this way:

"Be kinder to yourself. And then let your kindness flood the world." [5]

#2: Kindness is *not* weakness.

Kindness is sometimes seen as weak or wimpy, but it is not that at all. In fact, it is often the most difficult choice we can make.

Consider, for example, how hard it is to be kind when you're having a crappy day, when you're in a rush and stressed out, when someone is rude or unkind to you, or when someone does something you totally don't understand that annoys the hell out of you. For example, it's challenging for me to be kind to my husband when I have a sinus headache.

Also consider how easy it is to be unkind to yourself when you've screwed up. Or how challenging it is to speak out about something you believe to be unjust when your opinion is unpopular. "Tenderness and kindness are not signs of weakness and despair," says writer Kahlil Gibran, "but manifestations of strength and resolution." [6] And that is empowering, indeed!

#3: Kindness is *not* indulgence.

It's important to note that a kind act does not always feel good in the moment. If your child wanted to skip doing her homework and eat ice cream for dinner every night, it would not be kind to let her do so. This would be *indulgence*, which means doing something for someone that will make the person feel good in the moment but which leads to future unhappiness. Kindness, on the other hand, involves acting out of care and concern for someone's best interest—which isn't always immediately pleasant.

#4: Kindness is *not* just for humans.

Just as you can treat people kindly or unkindly, you can do the same with the earth and animals. In the book *A Plea for the Animals*, Buddhist monk and author Matthieu Ricard stresses that if we truly believe in kindness and ethical conduct, then the "right to live and not suffer cannot be the exclusive privilege of human beings."[7] I remember feeling so heartened when I watched my sister, Michelle, rescue a baby bird that had been knocked out of its nest by a wayward kite. She put on gloves before carefully picking up the tiny bird and climbing the tree one-handedly to nestle the bird back into its home.

Exercise: Kindness in Practice

Kindness begets kindness, which means that by simply reading about people performing acts of kindness, you'll be inspired to be kinder yourself. As you read the following stories, see if one inspires you in particular and if you can do something similar to put kindness into practice in your own daily life.

- Anja's neighbor, Lily, collected garden gnomes and proudly displayed them in her front yard and backyard. While Anja was searching online for plush toys for her dog, she came across a small gnome dog toy and thought Lily would get a kick out of giving this toy to her own dog, Rocky. Anja purchased the toy and left it anonymously on Lily's mailbox for her to discover.

- When she lost her job, Sherry began taking a lot of walks to pass the time. Once while on a walk she noticed a palm-sized smooth stone brightly painted with the words "Life is beautiful" under a tree. Seeing this positive message from a stranger made Sherry's day, but the kindness didn't stop there. Over the next few weeks, dozens of painted rocks appeared around her neighborhood, many with inspirational messages like "You matter"; "Hope"; and "Just breathe." Sherry never found out who did this kindness, but she hopes that whoever did it knows how much these messages meant to her.

- I heard author and speaker Emily Bennington share this inspiring story on the *Exploring a Course in Miracles* podcast.

   After being a manager for a long time, Bob was put in a position where he had to start answering to other people. This angered him and he became aggressive with everyone at the office, but especially with his own team. He turned his team sour on the organization as a whole, and they became challenging to work with.

   Scott, a manager who was at odds with Bob's group, went to his own team and told them, "We are not going to win by meeting Bob at the level of his aggression. So what we are going to do is show him and his whole team extreme courtesy and kindness. I know this will take you lifting yourself up above what you think you are capable of and it will take a long time, but if you trust this process, you will see results." It took six months, but it worked! Due to Scott inspiring his team to meet aggression with kindness, his team was able to shift the interactions with Bob's team into something more collaborative.

· When she was fourteen, Olivia was moved with compassion for the homeless people she saw around her hometown. So she began making care packages with the following items: socks, granola bars, raisins, toothpaste, toothbrushes, wipes, tissues, pads, soap, hand sanitizer, shampoo, conditioner, lotion, and dog treats. She kept these care packages in her family's car and gave them out whenever she came across a homeless person.

· Pat's oldest son, John, became ill with leukemia and despite all efforts wasn't getting better. When he knew he was dying, John told his wife that he did not want anyone to spend any money on flowers in his memory and preferred if those attending his funeral could bring whatever food they could afford to donate. John wanted the food to be given to the Oregon Food Bank, where he had been volunteering his time for the past few years.

When Pat and her husband, Sid, went to their son's funeral service, the whole sacristy area of the church was full of canned and packaged food. In fact, there was so much food that it took several truckloads to get it all to the food bank! When Pat shared this story with me, she said, "This showed what kind of a person John was. I was so proud of him, and so was his dad."

• While honeymooning in Europe, newlyweds Ruth and Dave were unable to sit together on a flight from Austria to France. Dave struck up a conversation with his seatmate, Francois, and by the end of the two-hour flight the two had made such a genuine connection that Francois even invited the newlyweds to visit him at his home in Paris during their travels.

A few days later Dave sent a text to Francois to let him know the days they would be in Paris. Francois responded that he and his wife both had to travel for work on those days, so he wouldn't be able to see them. Then he shared the jaw-dropping news that he wanted to give the honeymooning couple the gift of staying in his apartment *gratuit* (free) for the days they were spending in Paris. Ruth and Dave were overwhelmed with gratitude for Francois's generosity, especially after they entered the ancient apartment building and found that it was only seven blocks from the Notre-Dame Cathedral.

This chapter has explored many of the nuances of kindness, but there's another one, a big one, that we'll explore in the next chapter.

CHAPTER 2

Why Being Kind Makes You (Not Just Others) Happy

When you carry out acts of kindness you get a
wonderful feeling inside. It is as though
something inside your body responds and says,
"Yes, this is how I ought to feel."

—Harold Kushner

There are certain facts in life, and I'd like to offer to you this one: you want to be happier, and just like you, everyone else wants to be happier too.

Knowing that you're not the only one in the world who wants to be happier may make you feel a little better. There's a certain comfort in recognizing this. But there's another aspect to consider, one that may cause some of us to think—due to life circumstance or biology or some other reason—*Is it really possible to be happier?*

According to Sonja Lyubomirsky, professor of psychology at the University of California, Riverside and author of the bestselling book *The How of Happiness*, the answer is YES![8] For over twenty-five years, Lyubomirsky has been researching what kind of strategies people can use to increase happiness. She has found that not only can happiness change over time, but that kindness is a powerful intervention for boosting happiness. Other researchers have come to the same conclusion, and the result is that there is a large body of scientific research that suggests that being kind makes you happier.

Before we delve into this research a bit more, let's define what is meant by happiness here—just like we did with kindness at the start of this book. Well-being researchers generally define happiness as consisting of two components. The first component is *life satisfaction*, which is having a sense that our life is generally good; that we are adequately progressing toward our life goals and that we're fairly satisfied with our life.

But that's not enough. To be truly happy, we also need a second component, and that is the experience of frequent positive emotions—joy, serenity, enthusiasm, and pride, for instance—and the experience of less frequent negative emotions—sadness, anxiety, and anger, to name a few.

It is important to note that while happiness is associated with less frequent negative emotions, this does not indicate an *absence* of them. Even the happiest people feel sad when they lose someone they love, get frightened when there's danger, or feel angry when they're mistreated. A generally happy person experiences the full spectrum of emotions just like anybody else, but the ratio of their positivity to negativity may differ from less happy people.

Give Yourself Permission to Be Human

Please note, dear reader, that there's nothing inherently good or bad about any emotion. Louis and I want to reinforce this because believing that there are "good" and "bad" emotions may become a problem if and when we feel bad about ourselves for feeling a "bad" emotion.

So, for example, if you get angry and you believe this is a "bad" emotion, then this can make you believe that you're a "bad" or "terrible" person. Or if you're worried about something you believe you shouldn't be worried about, then this could make you think you're being irrational or overdramatic. These and other shame messages can run rampant through our minds, all because we aren't feeling the way we *think* we should.

Well, my friend, there are no "shoulds" when it comes to emotions: everyone, even the happiest people, experience negative emotions! In fact, to experience happiness, we first need to allow unhappiness. Happiness requires *the permission to be human*, which means allowing ourselves to experience *all* emotions, including painful ones.

Now that we've defined happiness, let's dive into the research! If you want to be happy, be kind. This is what Oliver Curry from the University of Oxford and his associates found after combing through more than four hundred published papers that investigated the relationship between kindness and happiness.[9] In this research, Curry found twenty-seven studies that explicitly tested this claim and then conducted a meta-analysis to statistically combine the results of these previous studies. The finding was that doing a kind act has a significant positive effect on well-being!

What's more, being kind to *anyone* boosts happiness. A 2019 study in the *Journal of Social Psychology* tested whether performing different types of kindness activities had differential effects on happiness.[10] The results indicate that being kind to anyone (yes, even ourselves) as well as simply actively observing kindness in action significantly boosts a person's happiness.

Did you know that kindness can boost your happiness in as few as ten days? In a study led by Kathryn Buchanan from the University of Kent, participants were asked to take a survey measuring life satisfaction.[11] They were then assigned to one of three groups. One group was asked to perform a daily act of kindness for the next ten days. Another group was told to do something new each day over the same ten days. A third group performed no acts. After the ten days were up, the participants completed the life satisfaction survey again. The findings were these: the groups that practiced kindness and did something new both experienced a significant boost in happiness; the third group didn't get any happier. This suggests that kindness does in fact make people happier—even when performed over as few as ten days. And there may be particular benefits to *varying* our acts of kindness, as novelty appears linked to happiness as well.

Kindness has even been shown to boost your happiness *more* than doing pleasurable activities like eating ice cream or buying a new pair of shoes. A study led by Michael Steger, director of the Laboratory for the Study of Meaning and Quality of Life at Colorado State University, found that those who engaged in behaviors such as "Volunteered my time," "Gave money to a person in need," or "Listened carefully to another's point of view" were happier than those who "Had sex purely to get pleasure," "Bought a new piece of jewelry or electronics equipment just for myself," or "Went to a big party."[12]

The kind act of spending money on others may be a surefire way to make yourself happier. This was the finding of a study led by Elizabeth Dunn from the University of British Columbia.[13] Dunn asked 632 participants to rate their general happiness, report their annual income, and estimate how much they spent in a typical month on (1) bills and personal expenses, (2) gifts for themselves, (3) gifts for others, and (4) donations to charity. The results showed that those who spent the most money on others were the happiest. Least happy were those who spent the least on others. It appears the more we give, the happier we become.

As you can see, research strongly supports the old adage "in giving we receive."

Why Kindness Boosts Happiness, Distilled

The reasons that being kind makes you happy are multiple. First: kindness simply feels good. In fact, kindness feels really good, as research suggests that it activates the same pleasure centers of the brain that are activated by food and sex (and who doesn't like having *those* pleasure centers activated?).[14] But happily, there is a difference in the duration of the joy you experience from pleasures—like eating a doughnut—and from being kind—such as talking to a person at a party who attended the event alone. According to Steger's previously mentioned research, the mood boost from pleasures is short lived—so once that doughnut is gone, your happiness quickly fades. The joy generated from kindness, however, lingers for hours, and often into the next day, after the kind act.

The second reason is that being kind gets your focus off your own issues and problems. The thing is, we spend much of our time thinking about ourselves. *(Life is all about ME!)*

This is especially true when you're feeling down: you get stuck in your head listening to a monologue about how crappy and awful your life is, and how crappy, stupid, and ineffective you are. But as Emiliya Zhivotovskaya, a leading voice in positive psychology, tells us, "Performing a kind act gets people into an 'other-centered' way of being, which can increase their mood, and put them into an upward spiral."[15]

Third: Being kind can "jump-start a cascade of positive social consequences," writes Lyubomirsky in *The How of Happiness*. "Helping others leads people to like you, to appreciate you, to offer gratitude."[16] (In fact, these are all things I noticed when I began purposefully practicing kindness, so if you need to, look back at the introduction again.) Research also suggests that being kind may lead people to be there for *you* when you're struggling.[17]

Exercise: Notice the Impact of Being Kind

Take a moment to bring to mind someone you know who is having a hard time. Now imagine something you can do that could be helpful. It could be just a few kind words, or it could be something you give to them that they might like.

Now imagine the person in some way being uplifted because of your kindness. As you imagine them being uplifted, notice what it feels like in your body and in your heart.

Fourth: It's likely that kindness can help with depression.

A five-year multidisciplinary study called the "Science of Generosity Initiative" by Christian Smith and Hilary Davidson of the University of Notre Dame suggests that being kind protects us from depression. In their book *The Paradox of Generosity*, they share this key finding of their study: "The more generous Americans are . . . the less likely and frequently do they suffer depressive symptoms."[18]

Researcher Neal Krause and associates of the University of Michigan's School of Public Health conducted a study to assess whether providing informal support to people who did not live with the study's participants—through bringing them meals, driving them somewhere, or shopping for them—would benefit the study's older help providers.[19] The research found that these older helpers, as compared to nonhelpers, experienced a measurably greater sense of personal control and reduced feelings of depression.

In fact, several studies have also shown a clear association between volunteering and reduced depression for older adults. A study led by Kathleen Hunter from the University of Miami School of Medicine compared volunteer workers over sixty-five with retired elderly who did not volunteer.[20] Volunteers were found to have significantly fewer symptoms of depression. Another study led by Marc Musick from the University of Texas found that adults over sixty-five who did regular volunteer work had fewer symptoms of depression than those who didn't.[21]

Studies like this give weight to physician, comedian, and author Patch Adams's suggestion, "Go out and serve and see your depression lift."[22] And that is exactly what Hannah experienced.

Hannah's Story

After graduating from college, Hannah realized her dream of moving to New York City and becoming a writer. Instead of this making her happy, however, she began to feel sad and lonely. It got so bad that she had trouble getting out of bed in the morning. She didn't want to face the day because she felt depressed and worthless.

Then one day while on a train, Hannah sat across from a woman who looked downtrodden and defeated. Hannah's heart went out to this woman, and she wanted to do something. Not knowing what else to do, she pulled out her notebook and started writing the stranger a letter, in which she expressed compassion and care for this woman she did not know.

Hannah wrote passionately for about ten minutes before looking up to see that the woman was gone. Hannah was disappointed, but she also noticed that she felt happier than she'd felt in a long time. She realized that despite her own depression, she could be there for someone else who was suffering—and that felt good!

It actually made Hannah feel so good that she decided to write letters like this as much as possible. Hannah began writing love letters and leaving them in random places around New York City for strangers to discover. She also posted on her blog that she would write a handwritten letter to anyone who requested it for any reason—no questions asked.

The letter requests poured in, and Hannah wrote back to everyone. It filled her heart with joy to do this. And the more she wrote to others, the better she felt herself. In fact, her depression lifted completely.

As the letter requests increased, however, Hannah found it impossible to keep up. Her heart broke at the thought of leaving any letter unanswered, so she started the nonprofit The World Needs More Love Letters; the organization sends handwritten letters to people in need around the world.

Hannah now says, "I have never felt so much joy and happiness, and it's because my life isn't about me anymore."[23]

While it's wonderful that Hannah's depression lifted as a result of her kindness, bringing her all the way to happiness, it is also prudent to offer a medical disclaimer to you, dear reader: *If you are suffering from severe depression, it would be wise to consult your doctor or seek out the opinion of some other medical professional.* Talk with your treatment provider first to discover if your intended kindness practices fit with the treatment you are or will be receiving. Our hope is that the doctor or medical professional will clear the way forward for your intended kindness practices, since not only can being kind make you and others happy, but it has many other fringe benefits, like reducing stress and improving health.

For more about this, read on!

CHAPTER 3

The Benefits of Kindness

Kindness is a passport that opens doors and fashions friends. It softens hearts and molds relationships that can last lifetimes.

—Joseph B. Wirthlin

You have incredible power to affect your own life and the lives of others—positively *or* negatively. So choosing to think, say, and do kind things matters. One obvious reason is that it makes others happy, and as you learned in the last chapter, it also makes *you* happy. Happily, all this is just the tip of the iceberg.

Here are five additional benefits (can you believe there are more?) you can expect from being kind.

Kindness Benefit #1: Kindness Inspires Kindness

While walking to my car from a pet store one day, I observed a woman drop one of the shopping bags she was carrying. Not realizing she had dropped it, this woman kept on walking. That's when a twentysomething man ran from all the way across the parking lot just to retrieve this lady's bag and get it to her before she got into her car and drove away. I watched as the woman's hands flew to her heart with appreciation for this man's kindness. When the man turned around to cross the parking lot, he was beaming with happiness—and I noticed that I felt happier too! Watching this small kindness had warmed my heart and made me want to do something kind too.

It's likely that you too get a warm and fuzzy feeling in your heart when you see someone else perform an act of kindness. Psychologist and author Jonathan Haidt calls this good feeling "elevation," which he defines as "a warm, uplifting feeling that people experience when they see unexpected acts of human goodness, kindness, courage, or compassion."[24]

Elevation not only feels good, it also prompts us to *do* good. This was shown in a couple of experiments led by Simone Schnall of the University of Cambridge.[25]

In the first study, participants were shown either a neutral television clip from a nature documentary or an uplifting clip from *The Oprah Winfrey Show*. Those who watched the uplifting clip, which was designed to create feelings of elevation, were more likely to volunteer to help on another study.

In the second experiment, participants were again shown television footage to evoke an elevated mood. When participants finished watching the clip, they were told they could leave, even while a research assistant in the room appeared to have computer problems and needed help with another questionnaire. Those participants shown the uplifting clip spent nearly twice as long helping out the research assistant before leaving the room.

These studies suggest that even a short exposure to others being kind elevates our mood *and* motivates us to act altruistically. But guess what? It doesn't stop there!

A study conducted by James Fowler from the University of California, San Diego and Nicholas Christakis from Harvard demonstrated that kindness is contagious.[26] In this study, participants were asked to play a game where selfishness made more sense than cooperation. While playing this game, when one participant chose to give money to help others, the recipients of those funds turned out to be more likely to give their own money away to other participants in future games. It was a "cascade effect," in which one person's kindness spread to numerous other individuals in subsequent games, generating a chain reaction of goodness. This suggests that a *single act of kindness can directly lead to dozens more!*

The Kindness Boomerang

In 2011, founder of the nonprofit organization Life Vest Inside, Orly Wahba, posted a video called "Kindness Boomerang – "One Day." It portrays how one kind act passes from one person to the next and boomerangs back to the person who set it in motion. In the video, Wahba explains that each incident was based on real moments of kindness that left a lasting impression on her life. Within months after its release, "Kindness Boomerang" went viral, reaching over twenty million people.[27]

Kindness Benefit #2: Kindness Is an Antidote to Stress

If you're feeling stressed out from juggling work, family responsibilities, and other commitments, you're not alone: in modern times, we all feel overwhelmed once in a while. But if you're regularly under stress, then your physical and emotional health can suffer.

According to the mayoclinic.org article "Stress Management," "Stress that's left unchecked can contribute to many health problems, such as high blood pressure, heart disease, obesity, and diabetes."[28] A growing body of research also suggests that chronic stress can have a negative impact on emotional health. A 2018 survey conducted by the Mental Health Foundation, for example, found that of those adults who felt stressed, 51 percent reported feeling depressed, and 61 percent reported feeling anxious.[29]

It is therefore important to reduce the stress we feel, hence the reason people are seeking out meditation, yoga, and other methods for reducing the impact of stress.

What works to reduce stress for my sister-in-law, Maria, a teacher and the mother of three (including two boys with autism), is to reach out to other moms of kids with autism. She told me, "Being there for other moms always reduces my stress and makes me feel better. Being kind to others and helping others ends up helping me even more." Maria's experience is not surprising, since a growing body of research suggests that being kind might be an effective stress management practice.

In a study led by Elizabeth Raposa of Yale University School of Medicine, 77 participants received an automated phone call every evening for two weeks prompting them to record whether they had experienced any stressful events over the course of the day.[30] They were also asked to record kind acts they performed that day, such as asking someone if they needed help, holding open a door, helping someone with their homework, and so on. Finally, participants were asked to rate the extent to which they were experiencing different positive and negative emotions, and their mental health for the day. Raposa found that *those who reported more acts of kindness experienced less negative emotion and less stress.* Even when some of them reported a number of stressful events, when they also reported a lot of small kindnesses on the same day, the stressful events had little or no impact on their emotions or sense of well-being! And when it came to those days when they didn't report as many kindnesses, the participants experienced more negative emotion in response to stressful events.

A massive survey of 3,300 volunteers conducted by Allan Luks, one of the top experts on volunteerism, also found that helping others reduces stress. In *The Healing Power of Doing Good*—a classic title where Luks documents the findings of this survey—Luks writes, "These dedicated volunteers experienced an enhanced, physical good feeling during the helping, followed after by a relaxed calmness marked by a heightened sense of self-worth that could last hours if not the rest of the day. The personal reports showed that these physical and emotional sensations appeared to significantly reduce daily stress."[31]

Kindness can even relieve travel stress according to a 2019 survey by Dignity Health.[32] While most people (82 percent of those surveyed) considered traveling to be stressful, the survey revealed that kindness can have a powerful effect on our happiness while in transit. In fact, the survey found that nearly all travelers (97 percent) agreed that being kind to others, as well as receiving kindness from others, can improve their overall well-being.

Over half the people surveyed said performing a gesture of kindness while traveling increased their happiness after performing the act. An even more encouraging finding from the survey? Kind acts can be truly tiny. A kind act as small as smiling or asking another traveler about their day can make a big difference in another's well-being. In fact, most travelers (66 percent) felt less stressed when another traveler simply smiled at them.[33]

Did you know that even being kind to yourself may help you handle stress better? A study published in *Health Psychology Open* found people who have higher levels of self-compassion tend to experience less of a physical stress response to challenging situations such as being stuck in traffic, having an argument with their spouse, or not getting that job offer they hoped for—and they spent less time reactivating stressful events by dwelling on them.[34]

Kindness Benefit #3: Kindness Is Good for Our Health, Whether We're Giving Kindness or Receiving It

Being kind goes beyond diffusing stress; it's also good for our health, and it even can reduce the physical pain we are experiencing.

In the Luks survey of 3,300 volunteers, Luks concluded that *regular helpers are ten times more likely to be in good health than people who don't volunteer.* In *The Healing Power of Doing Good,* Luks writes, "I received reports from people who can specifically relate their helping activities to a wide range of health gains, such as fewer colds, diminished pain from lupus, fewer episodes of flu, lessened tendency toward overeating, quicker recovery from surgery, help with insomnia, fewer migraines, and a cure for stomachaches. The list could go on and on."[35]

Kindness is also good for the heart. In his book *The Five Side Effects of Kindness*, author David R. Hamilton writes, "Kindness is cardioprotective."[36] Cardioprotective? This basically means that it benefits the cardiovascular system (heart and arteries). It does this because acts of kindness, even acts of self-kindness, produce the hormone oxytocin, and oxytocin is responsible for a whole range of positive effects on the heart and arteries. More specifically, oxytocin causes the release of a chemical called nitric oxide in our blood vessels, dilating and expanding them. This reduces blood pressure, and reduced blood pressure ultimately means protection against heart attack and stroke.

The amazing thing about this is that we can switch on this cardioprotective effect by being kind to ourselves or others. Kindness is *very* good for the heart.

Kindness is also a good antidote to pain. My friend Liz, a social worker who runs support groups for mentally ill patients, for example, suffers from chronic back pain. On her first day back to work after a long vacation, Liz told me that her pain was especially bad. Despite this pain, she ran her first group—and it went well. Her patients seemed happy that she was back, and she felt like she really helped them with some challenging issues. When the group was over, Liz noticed that her pain was gone.

Some research studies have investigated the effects of kindness on pain. A study led by Paul Arnstein from Boston College showed that when patients suffering from chronic back pain assisted other pain sufferers, they experienced improvements in their own pain, disability, and depression.[37]

According to David Hamilton, "The pain-relieving power of kindness comes in part from the endogenous opiates, also known as endorphins. Research shows that these bind to cells in the part of the brain involved in transmitting pain, taking the place of the chemicals that transmit pain signals and so interrupting the transmission of pain signals through the brain."[38]

While giving kindness helps us health-wise, the reverse, as shown in *The Rabbit Effect*, is also true: receiving kindness is also good for our health. So kindness is good all around!

The Rabbit Effect

In 1978, Robert Nerem and associates conducted a study designed to establish the relationship between high blood cholesterol and heart health in rabbits. When they looked at their results, they found something curious: one group of rabbits had far better health outcomes than the others. How could this be possible if they were genetically similar and being fed the same high-fat diet?

After careful observation, it was discovered that the healthier rabbits were all being tended to by postdoctoral researcher Murina Levesque, who in addition to feeding them was also petting and talking to them. She was basically giving them love and kindness. This finding was too big to ignore, so the study was conducted again, this time with tightly controlled conditions when it came to kindness and compassion.[39]

The results were the same: the group of rabbits who were treated with kindness did far better health-wise than the other rabbits who weren't.

It turns out that these rabbit studies were just the introduction to a much larger story. After years of researching the science of compassion, Dr. Kelli Harding, an assistant professor of psychiatry at Columbia University Irving Medical Center, wrote *The Rabbit Effect: Live Longer, Happier, and Healthier with the Groundbreaking Science of Kindness.* The wealth of research Harding shares in her book suggests that kindness really matters for our health and well-being. "It's not just one study; there is ample, ample evidence," shared Harding while being interviewed about her book on the *Live Happy Now* podcast, ". . . where how we're treated in different situations and doing things that are kind for ourselves and others seems to be helpful."[40]

One study Harding shares in *The Rabbit Effect,* for example, has to do with the powerful impact of motherly love. This study was conducted by psychoanalyst Dr. Rene Spitz, who was horrified by the very high death rate (about one out of three kids died) in Austrian orphanages in the 1940s.[41] At the time it was thought that the cause of the high death rate was contagious diseases, so children were isolated in cribs away from one another. Yet Dr. Spitz worried that in trying to create a sterile environment, the orphanages were actually unintentionally harming children through emotional deprivation.

To see if this theory was correct, Dr. Spitz followed two groups of children during their first years of life. One group consisted of babies living in the sterile conditions of an orphanage. The second group of babies lived in a prison nursery near their mothers. Although other doctors were concerned that children at the prison were at high risk of death from overcrowding and disease, Dr. Spitz found the opposite: during the study, three to four out of every ten children in the orphanage died— and none of those who lived in the prison died.

Another study Dr. Harding shares in *The Rabbit Effect* examined the interplay between illness and daily hugs, a very simple act of kindness. First, researchers at Carnegie Mellon University surveyed 404 participants over fourteen consecutive days, asking about disagreements and hugs received. Next, they exposed volunteers to the common cold (in the name of science and, just possibly, a hundred bucks!). Then they monitored any symptoms volunteers had, such as mucus production, for five days. Those who got daily hugs were *32 percent less likely to get sick!*[42]

The knowledge of literally hundreds of studies like these prompted Harding to share in her book's conclusion:

The hug we give our spouse or child as we walk out the door in the morning may influence how he handles an unpleasant interaction at work or school. The friendly chat with a neighbor may help her be kinder to the man behind the register where she buys her coffee on her commute to work. If we offer encouraging or demeaning feedback to an employee, it may sway whether she decides to attend a night class to feed her brain or chooses to veg out in front of the TV after work. It may also influence how she treats her family when she arrives home, which may in turn affect their stress levels that evening. Ultimately, these simple actions add up to how well we all sleep at night. Which affects our health. And starts the cycle anew the next morning.[43]

Kindness Benefit #4: Kindness Looks Good on Us

Many of us struggle with our looks. Surveys show that the majority of women (including some girls as young as six) are unhappy with their bodies—not surprising in today's appearance-driven society. We're continually bombarded with retouched images of unnaturally thin models with unblemished skin, perfect hair, and gleaming white teeth.

With these impossible standards of beauty, it's no wonder we're obsessed with makeup, working out for the perfect body, Brazilian Blowouts, plastic surgery options—and the list goes on. Did you know, though, that there's a new approach to becoming prettier, and it's *kindness*?

It's true: kindness really does make us more attractive! That's the finding of a study led by Andrew Thomas from Swansea University in the United Kingdom, who found that the top quality both women and men look for in a long-term partner is kindness.[44]

The study compared the dating preferences of students from Eastern countries like Singapore and Malaysia and Western countries like Australia, Norway, and the UK. Students were given eight attributes on which they could spend "mate dollars"; the attributes were physical attractiveness, good financial prospects, kindness, humor, chastity, religiosity, the desire for children, and creativity. The trait the most dollars were spent on? Kindness.

Another study led by Yan Zhang of Huazhong University in China randomly divided 120 participants into three groups and asked each participant to rate sixty photos of unfamiliar women making neutral facial expressions.[45] The participants rated the same pictures again two weeks later. This time, however, one group was given positive personality captions, like "kindness" and "honesty," alongside the same photos. The second group was given negative personality descriptions, such as "meanness" or "dishonesty," alongside the photos. The third group was shown the same photos without any descriptors.

In the first round of photo ranking, all three groups had given similar attractiveness ratings. But in the second round—when descriptions were (in some cases) added to the same photos—the group shown the same photos with positive personality descriptors assigned the highest attractiveness ratings to the photos, while the group with negative personality descriptors ranked the photos less attractive than the positive group and the control group. The researchers wrote, "We find that what is good is beautiful."

Kindness Benefit #5: Kindness Improves Relationships

Who doesn't want to improve their relationships, whether romantic, familial, work, or friendship? Happily, there's a secret to great relationships . . . you got it, it's kindness. This is what Bill Chopik, associate professor of psychology and director of the Close Relationships Lab at Michigan State University, discovered after he spent over twenty years combing through data on 2,500 long-term married couples. His research involved self-reported responses to questions about whether the couple had common interests and responses to the following five questions (which were used to evaluate their degree of five personality traits):[46]

1. "I am outgoing and sociable." (extraversion)
2. "I am considerate and kind to almost everyone." (agreeableness)
3. "I do a thorough job." (conscientiousness)
4. "I worry a lot." (emotional stability)
5. "I am original and come up with new ideas." (openness to experience)

Across the board, Chopik found that couples who reported higher levels of the personality trait of *agreeableness* (which means they are generally kind to others; number two in our kindness benefits list) reported being happier with their relationships. Surprisingly, having common interests or similar personalities didn't have very much effect on happiness at all. So it seems that while most of us invest a lot in finding a partner who's compatible with us, Chopik's research suggests that kindness matters way more in a relationship than having things in common.

Renowned psychologist John Gottman, famous for his work on relationships and marital stability, has shown that kindness is one of the most important qualities for successful relationships.[47] After videotaping thousands of couples and analyzing their interactions, Gottman argues that personal relationships are made up of an infinite number of small interactions, and that most of these can be seen as "bids for attention." Every bid for attention is an invitation for the other to "tune in," meaning to respond with warmth, interest, active listening, and empathy. Gottman found that happy couples "tune in" 86 percent of the time, while unhappy couples only do so one-third of the time.

In the end, Gottman found that we're happier in relationships when the other person offers us their caring attention more often (in other words, when they're being kind to us). This is as true in romantic relationships as in those with family, friends, and coworkers.

Research also suggests the obvious: that being kind helps us make friends. Kristin Layous, assistant professor of psychology at California State University, East Bay, and some of her associates conducted a study to investigate how kindness affects social standing and happiness.[48] Every week for four weeks, kids aged nine through eleven years old were asked to perform three acts of kindness or visit three places. Students in both conditions improved in terms of their own well-being, but those students who performed the kind acts also experienced significantly bigger increases in peer acceptance (i.e., popularity) than the students who visited places.

We've now learned about how kindness can truly benefit us and make us happier—but reading and learning is not enough to boost our well-being. It's the *practice* that has the transformative power. In the next chapter, you'll learn simple tips to make practicing kindness and generating overall happiness clear, successful, and easy.

CHAPTER 4

Just Why You Are Going to Succeed

Success is the sum of small efforts,
repeated day in and day out.

—Robert Collier

Practicing kindness is not something you do for a few weeks and then *voila!*—you're kinder and happier forever. It doesn't work that way: *an ongoing daily commitment is required for long-term gains.*

Does that sound a bit overwhelming? It's not, really. Remember, I learned that the best way to do this is by taking small steps (see the introduction)—and that's pretty easy.

In fact, a first small step you can take is *discovering your why*. After all, there's a reason you picked up this book. This reason, or your personal *why*, is very important. It is what will motivate you to begin practicing kindness—and continue practicing over time.

Let's start with what worked for me—because I think that just might work for you too!

It was discovering my *why*—that practicing kindness was a way for me to live in accord with my deepest value, which is kindness—that inspired me to take my first step into what was, for me, a "midlife opportunity." I recognized that despite how important kindness was to me, life often got in the way of living this value.

Then, when I found that practicing kindness also gave me a happiness boost, this became another *why*—icing on the cake! What's your *why*? Just *why*, in the first place, did you want to read about and practice kindness?

Here's an answer my friend Stevie courageously shared with me:

> The reason I want to learn kindness: Grew up in an abusive household with few examples of what kindness is. Watched my mother be miserable and didn't want to be like that. Kindness is a concrete example of how to live differently and be happier. I don't want to be abusive, but it's all I know. How do I *not* be this? This book can be a guide for those who never had guidance.[49]

Here are some other potential reasons. Do any resonate with you?
- Kindness is an important value for me.
- I want to be a role model for my kids.
- I'm not as happy as I'd like to be, and I want to

practice a science-informed method for becoming happier.

- There's so much negativity in the world—I want to "be the change."

Whatever the personal and specific reasons behind your *why*, they are important. Discovering your *why* is a vital first step on the road to becoming a kinder—and happier—person!

Exercise: What's Your *Why*?

Take a moment to think or write about your *why*. Here are some questions that may help as you reflect on the matter:

- Why did I pick up this book?
- What is most important to me?
- Why be kinder?
- What is the real reason I want to practice kindness?
- What are my most cherished values?

Five Tips to Help You Succeed on Your Kindness Journey

Now that you've hopefully had a bit of an epiphany and figured out just why you picked up—and stayed with (!)—this book, Louis and I want to provide a little "fuel" to help drive you forward on the practicing kindness journey you're about to embark on—that road that will transform you, transform others, transform the world, *and* make you happier. We have pulled together five tips to make sure your journey on the road to practicing kindness is successful—and continues.

Tip #1: Take small steps

A common mistake people make when attempting to change their behavior is *trying to do too much too fast*. While this may seem like a smart method, big changes are overwhelming and usually backfire. That's why Louis and I suggest cultivating the practice of kindness slowly. As I already discovered on my kindness journey, the best way to travel a thousand miles is not in one big single step (see the introduction).

You'll be more successful if you take small but consistent steps. The process works because small steps are easier to accomplish and repeat—so that they are more likely to become habits that transform your life! We like what Leo Babauta, writer of the Zen Habits blog, says:

"Make it so easy you can't say no."[50]

One way to take small steps is to focus on just one exercise explored in the second half of this book (part two) at a time. You might begin by doing an exercise from chapter 5 for one week, practicing an exercise from chapter 6 for the next week, and so on. It's also okay if you wish to keep trying the same kindness exercise for two or three weeks if that particular exercise continues to yield insights—or simply if you'd like to get better at it.

Know too that you can skip around and try out a specific exercise if it seems suited to the conditions of your life for a particular week. You don't have to go in order in the next part of the book. So, you can start with the exercises in chapter 5, but then try the exercises in chapter 11 next, if that is what appeals to you at the time.

Tip #2: Be playful

"Playing" is a helpful way to approach the practices of kindness we offer in the next section. Play is just a mindset, and we can be playful regardless of what activity we're engaged in. Being playful is important because it makes things exciting, fun, and adventurous. It's not about being frivolous or silly; it's about developing a sense of curiosity and wonder while you're working with these practices.

While being interviewed on the *Making Positive Psychology Work* podcast, happiness teacher and speaker Stella Grizont said, "We experience . . . that playful mindset . . . when we go traveling. We like to go traveling to a new destination; we like to go trying new restaurants."[51] You can bring that same attitude to becoming a kinder and happier person. *What are you going to discover today as you are being kind to another or yourself?*

Some of the exercises in this book may seem odd or too quirky to you—or even like they won't help you at all—but you can't really know unless you try them out. Being playful is about approaching these exercises with an attitude of *I wonder what's gonna happen?* instead of *Oh, I don't think this is gonna work for me!*

When I first heard about loving-kindness (see chapter 8), a practice that involves mentally sending myself and others loving phrases like "May you be happy," I didn't think it would be helpful at all. When I tried it, however, I found that it was powerful, and over time it's become an important part of my kindness practice.

It's true that sometimes you'll find that you enjoy or get more from an activity than you thought you would, while at other times the opposite will be true. Yet no matter what happens, it's good! It's all part of learning and self-growth.

Think back: As a child, you were literally a "play professional," right? You were intuitively curious and wondering. Well, how great would it be to tap into that energy once again? Louis and I want you to get intrigued about what you are going to discover in the pages that follow!

As you "play along" with these practices, you may find that they work better for you if you modify them. This is fine: you do you! Feel free to do whatever *you* need to do to make the practices your own so that you enjoy them and they inspire you.

Tip #3: Take failures lightly

Don't get down on yourself if and when you fail. An important key is to enjoy and not stress over practicing kindness. As cooking teacher Julia Child famously said, "If you drop the lamb, just pick it up. Who's going to know?" If you miss practicing for a day, a week, or a month, it's okay. Simply begin again.

An approach you might try instead of judging yourself when you fail to do a practice is to think about what you discovered. Sometimes *not doing* the practice will teach you more than doing it because you get to look at why you didn't do it. What was behind it: time pressures, feeling resistant to the exercise, or just forgetting? Such insights can help you make more conscious choices in the future. For example, if you discover that you are very resistant to doing a particular exercise, then maybe it's simply not a good fit for you. You will be learning lots of different exercises in this book just so you'll find the ones you personally connect with, so that means discovering one that doesn't fit is helpful too!

Another type of failure you're likely to run into is kind acts that backfire, like when you greet someone with a friendly hello and they don't greet you back, or when you bring dough-nuts to the office and later overhear your coworkers griping about the "annoying person" who tempted them to cheat on their diets (confession, this happened to me!). Try not to get discouraged when a kind act is unappreci-ated. The measure of appreciation shown by someone else does *not* determine the value of what you do. Your kind actions have intrinsic value; it's the thought that counts.

In the book *A Year of Living with More Compassion*, author and meditation teacher Susan Kaiser Greenland writes, "Genuine kindness requires us to focus on the goodness and wisdom of what we're doing rather than on the result and the less focus on the result the better we tend to feel."[52] Of course, it's also important to learn from these experiences: If your coworkers don't want doughnuts, then find other ways to be kind in the future.

One thing that may help you minimize kind acts that back-fire is to give *respectfully*. This means giving from a perception of equality with the other person (rather than seeing them as "less than") and being sensitive to others' feelings. My friend Janice, for example, told me how she once offered to help an elderly woman carry the two bags of groceries she seemed to be struggling with, and the woman snapped, "I don't need your help." At first Janice felt hurt, but as she thought about it, she realized that the woman was likely offended because she was being treated as needy. Giving respectfully is a nuanced art that we all get wrong sometimes, but you can get better at it by keeping in mind that sometimes kind acts aren't appreciated because it makes the other person feel needy or embarrassed; like you want something from them, think you're better than them, are coming on to them, or expect reciprocation in some manner when they may not want to reciprocate.

Tip #4: Practice with others

It can be fun and helpful to do kindness exercises with other people. As actress and director Amy Poehler said:

"Find a group of people who challenge and inspire you, spend a lot of time with them, and it will change your life."[53]

So, you might form a practice group that picks an exercise from this book to use for a week or two and then meets so you can all share what you've learned. You can also practice with others virtually by starting a Facebook group for those who want to purposefully practice kindness; tweeting about it; or connecting on another social media platform. Or you could do an act of kindness through purchasing this book for a friend to help them increase their happiness and reduce their stress, and then doing the practices together with them. (Want to really make them feel good? Slip a sticky note or handwritten card somewhere in the book telling them why you think they are so amazing.)

Tip #5: Keep a practice journal

To help you get the most out of this book, Louis and I recommend using a journal to record your experiences as you play with the practices. Writing can be helpful for self-growth because it allows you to deeply understand your thoughts, experiences, feelings, and ideas. As self-help guru Deepak Chopra claims:

"Journaling is one of the most powerful tools we have to transform our lives."[54]

And this is so, so true! Several months into my own kindness journey I wrote, "One of the things I've learned in my kindness experiments is how vital keeping a journal is. Sometimes I don't even know what I learned or what I got out of the experience until I write about it."

Here are three journaling questions that may help you process the exercises in this book:

1. What did I notice during that exercise?
2. How can this have practical value in my life?
3. How can I apply this exercise in my daily life?

Wonder what you will uncover and discover about yourself once you start writing? Let's figure that out—starting today!

Now that Louis and I have shared with you *why* we (and you!) got started, and how you can succeed, it's time to start doing! In the next part of this book, you will learn a variety of fun, simple, life-changing, and we believe *world*-changing, kindness practices. You can be the change—yes, YOU!

PART 2

Practice It!

CHAPTER 5

Find a Friend in You

Love is the great miracle cure. Loving ourselves
works miracles in our lives.

—Louise L. Hay

While being interviewed on *The Kindness Podcast*, radio host and podcaster Lisa Williams shared her experience about messing up on a radio show in Orlando: "When I came off the air," she recalled, "I threw my headphones against the wall and shouted aloud, 'That was so *stupid!*'" After watching this display, her producer looked at her and said, "Do not speak to yourself like that again." His words "really struck," said Lisa, "and I began a process where I started choosing to be kind to myself."

Years later Lisa had an experience where she spilled something on the kitchen floor. As she was cleaning up the huge mess, she heard herself say aloud, "It's okay, everybody makes mistakes." She recalled thinking, "Wow, Lisa, you have come full circle, because you were the girl who used to throw your headphones in disgust with yourself and chew yourself out with vile language. And now you're saying out loud to yourself on the kitchen floor, 'It's okay.'"[55]

Have you learned how to be your own friend like Lisa has? Consider this: If a good friend told you about a big mistake she made or something she's struggling with, how would you respond? Chances are you would offer her some words of comfort in a kind and soothing tone; perhaps you might give her a hug. Now, consider how you treat yourself when you are having a difficult time, fail, or don't like something about yourself. It's likely that you're harsh with yourself and jump to self-critical thoughts like, *I'm such an idiot!*

While we tend to treat our friends with love and compassion, we're incredibly hard on ourselves when we make a mistake or notice some flaw or shortcoming. And it's not without consequences: "Insecurity, anxiety, and depression are incredibly common in our society, and much of this is due to self-judgment,"[56] writes Kristin Neff, a professor at the University of Texas at Austin and a pioneer of self-compassion research. In fact, research suggests that self-criticism contributes to depression, anxiety, eating disorders, substance use disorders, and physical health conditions.[57]

What's more, we know how much it hurts. Thinking things like, *I'm a loser. I'm such a screwup! I'm worthless. There's something inherently wrong with me. I'm an idiot! I'm not good enough*, are psychological punches that make us feel battered. So why do we do it?

I don't know about you, but when I ask myself this question, instead of answering it, I start beating up on myself for being so mean to myself instead! ☺ That's why I was thankful when

I read Neff's suggestion: "Don't beat yourself up for beating yourself up in the vain hope that somehow it will help you stop beating yourself up. Instead, take a step back, and give your inner critic some slack. In its ineffective, counterproductive way, your inner critic is actually trying to keep you safe."[58]

It's true: our inner critic believes it is doing what is necessary to ensure our success and safety. It thinks that being harsh is the best way to motivate us to improve and prevent future mistakes so that we will remain safe, loved, and accepted.

Thus, our inner critic is not our enemy; it's simply misguided. Its tactics don't work. On some level we know this: we are aware that its cutting words don't encourage us to succeed or boost our confidence, in the same way we recognize that it isn't helpful for a teacher to belittle a child and that it's not okay or helpful for us to call our friends nasty names. And yet for some reason, our inner critic didn't get the memo that being harsh to ourselves is not helping us.

So what's a better way? To treat ourselves with the same gentleness, understanding, kindness, and compassion we would show to a good friend!

As an example, let's say you're on a diet and you slip up and eat too much pizza and cake at a friend's party. Instead of saying to yourself, *I'm disgusting, I can't believe I did that. I'll never lose weight*, talk to yourself in a warm and encouraging way like you would to a friend. You might in a comforting tone say, *Hey, you know what? I screwed up a little bit. But I did follow my diet pretty well for the past week, and I'll get back on track.*

Contrary to what the inner critic would have us believe, when we are kind to ourselves, we become not only happier but also more successful in life. New research suggests self-kindness may be a superior way to motivate ourselves and achieve our goals.[59] Nurturing and encouraging ourselves gives us the support we need in the face of failure, and this allows us to learn from our mistakes and bounce back with greater enthusiasm.

The power of self-kindness goes beyond boosting our happiness and success; it actually alters the brain and body at a cellular level. When you respond to your failures and struggles in a caring and comforting way, your body releases the feel-good hormone, oxytocin. Research has shown that increased levels of oxytocin reduce fear and anxiety and strongly increase feelings of trust, calm, contentment, generosity, and empathy. Oxytocin additionally inhibits the release of stress hormones such as cortisol.[60]

Self-kindness has additional benefits too. Research suggests that people who are kind and compassionate with themselves are much less likely to be depressed, stressed, and anxious, and are much more likely to be happy, resilient, and in better physical health.[61] Other positive effects of self-compassion suggested by study findings include the following:

- It is linked with greater psychological well-being.[62]
- It is linked with stable feelings of self-worth.[63]
- It may help you achieve your weight loss goals.[64]
- It increases motivation.[65]

Shattering Shame

One thing that sometimes gets in the way of finding a friend in ourselves is *shame*—which shame and vulnerability researcher Brené Brown describes as "the intensely painful feeling or experience of believing we are flawed and therefore unworthy of love and belonging."[66]

Shame is a normal human emotion, and it is also one of the most painful emotions we can experience. When we are feeling shame, our thoughts tend to be focused on the belief that something is wrong with us.

Shame can sometimes serve a purpose, such as preventing us from behaving in ways that may cause others to reject us or alerting us when we are doing something that doesn't align with our values. Other times, however, shame doesn't have any useful purpose, and it may arise from internalizing past experiences of being devalued, humiliated, or abused. Feelings of shame are not problematic unless we get stuck in them or respond in unhelpful ways.

As an example, I spent a large portion of my life stuck in shame due to my debilitating social anxiety. I believed that because it was incredibly challenging for me to talk to people or even make eye contact with others, there must be something inherently "wrong" with me. I felt so ashamed of my shyness that I tried to hide it from everyone, fearing that if anyone found out, they'd reject me. My deep feelings of shame prevented me from living a full life and finally plunged me into a depression.

I wanted to get help, but that meant I'd have to tell someone about my debilitating social anxiety—the last thing I wanted to do, because then someone would know how horrible and unlovable I was! Interestingly, when I finally told a therapist about my painful shyness, I felt like a huge weight had been lifted. I'd revealed my secret, so it wasn't as heavy of a burden anymore. "If we cultivate enough awareness about shame to name it and speak to it," says Brené Brown in her book *Daring Greatly*, "we've basically cut it off at the knees."[67]

If you feel like you're stuck in shame that's preventing you from being your own friend or having compassion for yourself, one approach that may help you get beyond it is acknowledging it and sharing your experiences with the trusted people in your life or with a mental health professional. By sharing your shame, you are refusing to let it define you.

"When we bury the story we forever stay the subject of the story," writes Brown. "If we own the story we get to narrate the ending."

Even if we recognize the benefits of treating ourselves like a pal, our inner critic has been beating up on us for a long time. Is it even possible to change? Yes! Our brains are incredibly plastic, or able to change and adapt, and that means your inner critic is changeable. You *can* learn to be kind and compassionate with yourself. You can learn to treat yourself as you would a friend whom you see fall into a funk after a bad breakup. And for that, you've earned a round of applause!

Exercises

Exercise #1: Try speaking kindly to yourself.

One of the most important ways you can befriend yourself involves changing your critical self-talk. Speaking unkindly to yourself is likely so normal that you may do it without even realizing it! Thus, a first step is to simply notice when you're beating up on yourself.

Every day this week, make it a point to notice when you are speaking harshly to yourself. When you do, ask yourself: *Would I say this to a friend or someone I care about?* If the answer is no, think about what you would say to a friend in the same situation. And then just try it out with yourself.

As motivational author Louise Hay said,

> *"Remember, you have been criticizing yourself for years, and it hasn't worked. Try approving of yourself and see what happens."*[68]

Notice how it feels to speak kindly to yourself. At first it may feel awkward or fake—and that's okay. Whenever you try something new, it feels unusual at first. The more you practice this, however, the more comfortable and comforting it will become.

Exercise #2: Gain distance from your inner critic thoughts.

Imagine that after blowing a job interview, you tell a friend, "I'm such an incompetent loser; I'll never get a job." Is she going to believe you? No way! A good friend is not going to take your self-judgmental thoughts seriously, and you can learn to do the same.

One way to do this is to recognize that our thoughts are just thoughts, not facts. They are just words going through our mind. We are not those thoughts—we can defuse ourselves from them.

Whenever you recognize the voice of your inner critic this week, pull out a scrap of paper and write down your negative, self-judgmental thought. For example, *I'm stupid* or *I'm boring.*

Now mentally replay the thought with this phrase in front of it: *I'm having the thought that . . .* For example, *I'm having the thought that I'm stupid.*

There is a massive difference between thinking, *I'm stupid and boring,* and thinking, *I'm having the thought that I am stupid and boring.* This shift helps us create distance between the thought and us and observe the thought more objectively like a friend would do for us.

Exercise #3: Write an encouraging letter to yourself.

A challenging time to be your own friend is when you are struggling with something that is causing you to feel shame, to feel insecure, or to feel like you're not "good enough." While imperfection is the nature of being human, many of us treat ourselves harshly for our human challenges and imperfections.

This week, try writing a letter as if you were talking to a beloved friend who is struggling with the same concern you are struggling with (such as a work or relationship issue, or judgment about your looks or perceived inadequacies). What words of support and encouragement would you offer to them?

Once you complete the letter, go back and read it, applying the words to yourself.

Exercise #4: Try a "selfie hug"!

If a friend is feeling bad, you'd likely offer her a hug. To be your own friend, why not try giving yourself one? This may sound strange, even silly, but your body doesn't know that. It just responds to physical touch—even your own touch—by activating your parasympathetic nervous system, helping you calm down and feel safe.

Whenever you're feeling anxious, upset, down, or self-critical this week, wrap your arms around yourself and give yourself a warm hug. You may find it helpful to also softly stroke your arms or gently rock your body. If other people are around and you don't want to do this in front of them, you can fold your arms across your body in a nonobvious way or simply imagine hugging yourself.

CELESTE'S JOURNAL ENTRY: Imperfect, Beautiful, and Loved

I had a red, itchy blotch the size of a nickel on my cheek, so I made an appointment with a dermatologist. She said, "This looks suspicious," and did a biopsy. It wasn't cancer, so she burned it with a laser and told me that it would fade away in a month or so. For the next week, I wore a bandage to cover most of the side of my face. When I took the bandage off, the spot was really, really red and looked much worse than it had before I saw the doctor! I felt self-conscious about it but comforted myself in knowing that it would fade away.

But it didn't fade away. Six months later the spot was still there; in fact, it had grown bigger, had developed irritated bubbles, and was still very red. I returned to the dermatologist and she told me she wanted to burn it again. She also told me that it was precancerous and that it could become cancerous if I didn't treat it right away. I felt unsure about repeating a treatment that seemed to make the spot worse, so I told the doctor I wanted to think about it for a few days.

I left the appointment upset. I thought, *Living with this blemish is horrible. I don't like going places and interacting with peo-*

ple when I look like this. People stare at me and judge. What's more, burning it the first time didn't help; what if doing it again doesn't help either? Then again, what if it does *become cancerous?* At some point in my pity party, I realized how harshly I was treating myself. Instead of offering myself care and concern, I was telling myself that my situation was awful and that people were judging me over my appearance. *That's not what I would say to a friend who was struggling in this way.*

I tried to imagine what I would say to a friend in this situation, but my mind kept jumping back to how awful things were for me. Since visualizing wasn't helping me, I tried something different—writing a letter to console my sister as if she were the one struggling with this issue. Here's that letter:

Dear Michelle,

I was so sorry to hear your concern and frustration over the blemish on your cheek. That must be very hard to deal with, and I feel for you. Almost anyone going through this situation would feel concern, frustration, and disappointment. This is really hard.

At the same time, I see you as so beautiful. Even with this blemish, you light up a room with your smile. You have such good energy that people love being around you. This imperfection doesn't diminish you at all. What's more, if you are able to "own it," you will inspire others with your strength of character.

While I know it feels like others are judging you, it's unlikely that anyone would judge you for this.

Sure, some people may notice, but not in a judging way. We are all imperfect, and our imperfections make us human. Just as you wouldn't judge someone else with such a blemish, others are unlikely to judge you.

I know that you are also frightened by the possibility of your blemish turning into cancer. That's understandable. Anyone would feel concerned by this. Still, if anyone can handle this, you can. You have so much strength. You have successfully dealt with so many challenging situations in your life, and you always get through just fine. You will get through this situation too. You got this!

And no matter what, just know that I love you. I love you right now, exactly the way you are. You don't have to change anything to have my love. I will always love you just the way you are. No matter how you look, nothing can change the beauty of your heart. You are just so beautiful.

Please know that I am here for you always. If you need anything, I'm here. And one more time to make sure that you remember, I love you!

Please take good care of yourself and be well.

Love always,

Celeste

After writing the letter, I read it aloud as if I'd written it to myself. This turned out to be so much more moving than I expected that by the end of it, I was bawling! I hadn't cried like that in years, and it felt good to really just let go.

Once I got my composure back, I felt better and more hopeful about my situation. As my letter reminded me, I *would* get through this.

I am so glad that I am my friend.

P.S. It turned out that the spot was cancerous after all, and I got through it just fine.

CHAPTER 6

Create "Micro-Moments" of Love

I see friends shaking hands, saying how do you do.
They're really saying, I love you.

—Louis Armstrong

When Louis was eight years old, he and his family moved to a new town. One of his most vivid memories is of his new neighbors knocking on the door their first night and welcoming his family to the neighborhood with a potluck meal. The previous neighborhood he'd lived in also had been a friendly community that held annual block parties with music and games.

Fast-forward to several months ago (as of this writing) when Louis bought a house in Southern California, and not one neighbor knocked on his door to welcome him! This probably doesn't surprise you: we've become accustomed to being less friendly with our neighbors. Today most of us either live in apartments without knowing who lives on the other side of our walls, or we enter our homes through the garage and hang out in our fenced backyards instead of chatting with people from the front porch like our grandparents did.

It's not just in our neighborhoods that we're less friendly—it's *everywhere*. In today's world, we've got digital devices and unending to-do lists that distract us from being friendly to the humans in front of us. So instead of smiling and greeting a store clerk or people walking by, we're monitoring email or returning text messages. Or instead of stopping to chat with a neighbor, we're rushing to our next appointment. And instead of listening to our friend, coworker, child, or partner, we're lost in thoughts about all the things we have to get done.

While it's easy to dismiss brief friendly connections as trivial, research suggests this is a consequential mistake because they fulfill a basic human need for love. Love—really? Isn't that a deep, ongoing feeling reserved just for soulmates and family ties? Not according to Barbara Fredrickson, the foremost researcher of positive emotions.

In her book *Love 2.0*, Fredrickson explains that love is an emotion—and like all emotions, it is *not* enduring. It arises for a moment and then subsides. Love, through this lens, can be experienced numerous times a day with different people ranging from family members to strangers we connect with in passing. Fredrickson calls these brief moments of shared connection from behaviors like smiling at someone, saying hello, stopping for a brief chat, or hugging someone "micro-moments of love," and her research suggests that such moments are vital to our health and happiness.[69]

"Love, as it turns out, nourishes your body," says Fredrickson. "The more you experience it, the more you open up and grow, becoming wiser and more attuned, more resilient and effective, happier and healthier."[70] Micro-moments of love can also strengthen relationships, even long-standing intimate relationships.

Although they are not always called "micro-moments of love," other research supports the positive benefits of brief social connections. In a study by social psychologists Gillian Sandstrom and Elizabeth Dunn, for example, participants were asked to go into a coffee shop and order a drink.[71] One group of participants was asked to smile, make eye contact, and have a brief conversation with the barista, while another group was asked to be as efficient as possible. It was found that the people who had a brief social interaction experienced greater happiness than people who were as efficient as possible.

Of course, micro-moments of love don't just affect you positively. They also affect the people you *share* them with, be that person your spouse, your parents, your child, or a casual acquaintance or stranger. Or that unknown neighbor you greeted while both of you were walking your dogs.

So, if you want to purposefully spread micro-moments of love, what can you do? Here's a list of suggestions, all of them requiring only a small amount of your energy, but large in the amount of love they'll be spreading:

- *Smile at everyone.* Your smile is one of the simplest yet most beneficial gifts you can give to your friends, your family members, and strangers.

When you smile at someone, you are showing them that they matter, which boosts their happiness. How cool is that?

Smiling also signals friendliness and encourages positive interactions. And smiling is *contagious*: when you smile at someone, mirror neurons in their brain compel them to smile back.

- *Greet people.* One way to do this is to follow the 10/5 principle that Louis is a firm believer in: If someone is within ten feet of you, acknowledge them with a wave, nod, or smile. When someone is within five feet, say hello.

- *Focus on who's in front of you.* Make a point to put down your digital devices and focus on the humans in front of you. When talking with another person, be it your partner, your child, a shop clerk, the woman who makes you coffee on Monday mornings, or the mechanic who services your car every few months, fully commit to that conversation, and listen to them with the same interest and passion that you wish others would listen to you with. Make them feel like the most important person in the world to you in that moment.

- *Introduce yourself to others.* Many of us are shy about meeting new people (I know I am), but it's worth mustering the courage to be the one to break the ice and introduce yourself to other people because it spreads love and creates friendships. Opportunities are endless: introduce yourself to a neighbor you've seen around but haven't met, the newbie at work, those you see while walking your dog, people at a religious service or social gathering, the person next to you on a plane, or someone behind you in line. Not sure how to introduce yourself? You can simply say, "Hi! I'm _____. What's your name?"

- *Make a casual comment to someone near you.* Pay attention to your surroundings and those around you, and make a friendly comment to someone about your shared space or experience. If you're waiting in a long line, for example, turn to the person next to you and say in a light and positive way, "Boy, this line is long today!" Or you could make a comment on the weather, how much you're enjoying the taco from the food truck, or the adorable golden retriever that just passed.

- *Give a sincere compliment.* When you notice something about someone else that you appreciate, share it. It doesn't matter whether you're commenting on their taste in music, their choice in clothes, or the way they did their hair; let them know you like what they did!

I once complimented a grocery clerk's lovely pink fingernails decorated with little cherries, and she beamed as she told me that she'd painted them herself. This brief exchange had me walking out of the store wearing a smile and feeling great. Make sure to keep your compliments genuine and respectful, however. You don't want to come across too strong or like you're hitting on someone (!).

- *Be curious about others.* Get to know others by asking open-ended questions that create dialogue rather than questions that could be answered with a "yes" or "no" or another one-word response. On my first date with my now husband, Paul, he asked me, "What do you think it would be like to have a movie made about your life?" I loved this question! It got me talking (and fantasizing) about my life being portrayed on the silver screen by Amy Adams, and our conversation flowed from there.

  Here are some curiosity questions you might try out:
  - "What shows are you into?"
  - "Have you been to any good restaurants lately?"
  - "Have you seen any good movies lately?"
  - "Where did you grow up?"
  - "What are you looking forward to?"
  - "Any upcoming travel plans?"
  - "What are you excited about?"
  - "What do you do for fun?"
  - "What is the craziest thing you have ever done?"
  - "Are you reading any good books right now?"
  - "What is your favorite childhood memory?"
  - "What's the most unbelievable thing that's ever happened to you?"

- "Who was your first crush?"
- "Do you collect anything?"
- "Who are the special people in your life?"
- *Give hugs.* The power of hugging is profound. In her book *The How of Happiness*, Sonja Lyubomirsky discusses a Pennsylvania State University study in which students were assigned to two groups. One group was assigned to give or receive at least five nonsexual hugs a day for four weeks to or from five different people. The second group, the control, was instructed to simply record the number of hours they read each day over the same four weeks. The results showed that the students in the hugging group became much happier, while the students who recorded their reading activity showed no changes.[72] Make an effort to hug more often. Perhaps even set a goal to give five hugs a day for a week and see what that's like for you (and for others!).

Exercises

Exercise #1: Reflect on your social connections.

Many of us miss out on potential micro-moments of love every day because we're oblivious or blind to them. That's why Fredrickson recommends preparing yourself to capitalize on opportunities for love when they arise. One way of doing this is by reflecting on your social interactions each day. This works because it serves as a gentle reminder that each social interaction is indeed an opportunity for something more than just an exchange of goods or information.

At the end of each day this week, call to mind your social interactions. As you think about these interactions, ask yourself how in tune you felt with the people you connected with. You may find it helpful to record your thoughts in a journal and observe whether your responses change over time.

Exercise #2: Create three micro-moments of love.

Every day this week, seek out at least three opportunities to really connect with others. Opportunities may arise at home, at work, in your neighborhood, or while you are out and about in your community. Wherever you are, be it at a store, a fair, or walking in your neighborhood, put down your phone and freely offer others your attention. Be friendly, make eye contact, greet people, show interest, engage in lighthearted conversation, say "thank you" at the end of an interaction, stay present when another person is speaking to you, and when appropriate, introduce yourself to others.

Exercise #3: Spread love at home.

Our family members are the most important people in our lives, but we don't always treat them that way. Instead, we may take them for granted, neglect them, or even treat them unkindly. You have the power to change that!

Every day this week, look for opportunities to create micro-moments of loving connection with your family members. Some ways you might do this are to hug often, say "I love you," tell them what you appreciate about them, greet them warmly when they come home, play a game with them, be fully present and attentive, support what they are doing, and ask about their day (and really listen as they share).

Exercise #4: Create a "culture of love" at work.

You don't need an office romance for love to bloom at work. Instead, seed love the micro-moments way!

Every day this week, seek out at least three micro-moments of love at your workplace. For example, you might warmly greet everyone at the office when you arrive in the morning, thank a colleague for helping you with a project, support what your coworkers are doing and do what you can to help them succeed, give another a sincere compliment, show interest in others, be affirming, introduce yourself to a newbie colleague, or engage in lighthearted conversation in the break room.

CELESTE'S JOURNAL ENTRY: The Power of a Smile

When I handed my license and ticket to the TSA agent at the Boston airport, I warmly greeted him and smiled. The agent surprised me by saying, "Thank you for smiling."

I didn't think my smile had been all that out of the ordinary, so his comment made me curious. I asked, "Is it unusual for people to smile at you?"

"Oh, yeah," he responded in a friendly way. "But we understand. It's just the nature of things around here."

I made focused eye contact with the man's striking blue eyes and said, "I hope you have a wonderful day." At this, he pulled up the strap blocking off an aisle and advised, "Why don't you and your husband go in this line? It's the shortest one."

"Thanks!" I said, feeling a little guilty because he was doing us this favor. I hadn't smiled at him so that he might be inclined to do anything special for us—yet I also knew it would be rude not to accept his kindness graciously. So that's just what I did.

This brief incident boosted my mood so much that when we got into the terminal, I wanted to do something to pay it forward. I asked Paul to sit with me for a moment while I pulled out a pack of sticky notes and wrote, *May you, yes you, the person reading this, be happy* ☺, on seven or eight of them. Then Paul and I walked around the terminal finding nooks to place the notes for people to discover them later on.

Even Paul seemed lightened by my happy mood: "I think what you're doing is pretty cool," he commented.

"Thanks, sweetie," I said.

How amazing it was that this ripple of good feelings and "paying it forward" all began with a simple smile! ☺

CHAPTER 7

Step Up Your Generosity

We live far happier lives when we are generous in as many ways as possible.

—Cathy Burnham Martin

Tonight was dessert night—the one night per week that Paul and I indulge in a decadent, fat-laden, sugary treat. *Yum!* All day long I had been looking forward to the vegan espresso chocolate chip cookies I'd picked up for tonight. Before I could gratify myself, however, I had to walk my pooch, Mambo.

While walking my dog, I ran into our neighbors, the Hobbs, and on a whim, I said, "Why don't you guys come over for a cold drink a little later?"

"Sure!" they answered. They said they'd stop by in an hour.

When I told Paul that we'd be having company, he said, "Do you want to share our cookies with them?"

"No," I responded immediately. I knew this was selfish, but

since dessert night was only once a week, I wanted to savor every morsel of those cookies. *Besides, I rationalized, they'd never even know we have cookies if we don't tell them.* Then I remembered—albeit with a disappointed sigh—that I was practicing being generous that week. So I knew what I had to do: I told Paul that I'd changed my mind and wanted to share the cookies.

I found the evening with our neighbors to be very enjoyable. Everyone chatted, laughed, savored cold drinks and cookies, and had great time.

When the Hobbs left, I knew I'd received a lot more pleasure from sharing than I would have gotten from eating alone.

⌒

That's the paradox of generosity: *giving good things away makes you happier than keeping them for yourself.* You've heard this before no doubt, as spiritual traditions and philosophers have been telling us this for centuries. St. Francis of Assisi said, "For it is in giving that we receive." And, "If you knew what I know about the power of giving," said the Buddha, "you would not let a single meal pass without sharing it in some way."

But did you know that science now backs up this claim? At the University of Notre Dame, researchers Christian Smith and Hilary Davidson have been studying *generosity*, which they define as "the virtue of giving good things to others freely and abundantly." For their research they did a massive survey of Americans' practices and beliefs about generosity, interviewed hundreds of Americans about generosity, and conducted participant-observation studies of local religious congregations. In their book *The Paradox of Generosity*, they write that their research strongly suggests that "the more generous Americans are, the more happiness, health, and purpose in life they enjoy."[73]

Other studies also suggest that generosity boosts happiness. In a study by social psychologist Elizabeth Dunn, for example, students on a university campus were given a five-dollar or twenty-dollar bill to spend by the end of the day.[74] Half the participants were instructed to spend the money on themselves, and the other half were asked to spend it on someone else. That evening, participants who spent the money on someone else reported feeling happier over the course of the day than those who spent it on themselves. Interestingly, the amount of money they got made no difference on their happiness level. It was the simple act of kind generosity that counted!

This experiment proves most of us wrong in our belief about what makes us happy—including the separate group in Dunn's study asked to predict outcomes of the experiment. Most of them believed those who spent money on themselves would be happier.

More proof that it's better to give than receive!

Generosity is powerful—and you don't have to be generous on a grand scale either. One way to practice is by *being generous in small ways*, like giving a dollar to a homeless person or to a charity at the grocery store, relinquishing your potential parking space to someone else, or sharing your cookies. Even the tiniest acts of generosity can really make a difference to someone else, boost your own mood, and help you become a true believer in the paradox of generosity.

Another way to practice generosity is by *being generous in larger ways*. For example, you might give a sizable donation to a charity or be generous with your time by volunteering for a nonprofit organization for several hours a week. Louis and I are not suggesting that you practice being generous in large ways from now on, but rather that you try it out once as an experiment and see what it's like for you.

A third method of practice is *to cultivate a mindset of abundance*. In her book *Lovingkindness*, mindfulness teacher Sharon Salzberg writes, "Generosity allies itself with an inner feeling of abundance—the feeling that we have enough to share."[75] With an abundance mindset, you acknowledge that there is plenty of happiness, success, wealth, and everything else we all may need; there's enough for you, and there's also enough to spare for everybody else. With this mindset, you *readily share with others*. You know that there is always enough for today and for tomorrow!

An abundance mindset actually has little to do with external wealth. Just think about this: there are rich people who find it difficult to give despite their external abundance. I have a friend of a friend who, despite inheriting a substantial fortune, doesn't tip more than 10 percent—ever. Conversely, there are economically poor people who give generously from the little they have.

Strangely, instead of an abundance mindset, many of us have a *scarcity mindset*, which means we tend to think there isn't enough for us, let alone enough to share. A scarcity mindset not only makes us stingy, but it also is unkind to our own selves because it makes us feel perpetually unsatisfied. We go through our days always wanting *more.*

If this is true of you, one way to cultivate an abundance mindset is to practice gratitude by noticing and appreciating the good things in your life. Two simple and effective gratitude exercises are:

- Writing down three good things each day
- Keeping a gratitude journal

By the way, research suggests that these gratitude exercises also boost happiness!

Exercises

Exercise #1: Step up your generosity.

Every day this week, make an effort to be more generous than you typically are. To do this, simply be on the lookout for small or large ways to be generous with time, money or goods, caring, etc.—and then act on them. Offer to help your older neighbor carry in their grocery bags; don't take the last close parking spot but park farther from the store so it's easier for that mom in the approaching minivan to get into the store with her infant or toddlers in tow. Or spend several hours volunteering at an animal shelter, food bank, or other nonprofit organization this week. The website VolunteerMatch.org can help you find volunteer information and listings in your local community.

Exercise #2: Donate to a worthy cause.

Make a small, or large, donation to a charity of
your choice this week. If you're not sure what
charity to give to, you can use websites like
GreatNonprofits.org, CharityNavigator.org, and
GiveWell.org that can help guide you toward making a meaningful donation.

Exercise #3: Write three good things.

As mentioned in this chapter, you can become
more generous by cultivating an abundance mindset by doing gratitude exercises. One powerful
gratitude exercise is to write down three good
things every day. Here's how to do it: Every day
this week at a regular time, such as right after
dinner or just before bed, write down three things
that went well during your day and how you contributed to these good things happening. These can
be simple and ordinary things, like enjoying a good
meal or receiving a compliment on your new hair-
style from a coworker, or relatively large things,
like getting a promotion or passing a test. Here are
some examples:

- "Really enjoyed lunch with Mary today. I haven't
  seen her for so long—it was wonderful to catch
  up. I contributed to this by reaching out to her
  last week."
- "Saw a striking sunset tonight. I contributed to

this by taking some much-needed 'me' time by going for a walk after dinner."

- "Hooray—I completed everything on my to-do list today. I contributed to this by not letting myself waste too much time on social media during the day."

Tip: If you continue this practice for more than one week, you may discover it's better for you to count your blessings only a few days a week rather than every day. Doing so can prevent boredom and monotony so that the exercise continues to yield benefits.

Exercise #4: Keep a gratitude journal.

Another gratitude practice that may help spark your generosity is to *keep a gratitude journal.* Do this at least one day this week by writing in depth about things you feel grateful for. There is no wrong way to journal, but here are some tips to keep in mind:

- **Get personal.** Writing about people you feel grateful for is often more beneficial than focusing on things you are grateful for. Who deserves your thanks today or this week?
- **Be specific.** The more specific you can get while writing what you are grateful for, the easier it is to connect with the emotion. For example, writing "I'm grateful that my partner cleaned the

kitchen while I was at yoga" is more powerful than "I'm grateful for my partner."

- **Mix it up.** Vary what you write about. If you write about the same blessings all the time, you're likely to become bored with the activity and get less meaning from it.

CELESTE'S JOURNAL ENTRY: Better Than a Happy Meal!

Paul and I spent the day driving home to Southern California after visiting my family in the San Francisco Bay Area. It had been a frustrating day so far: a few hours into the drive, we were in a fender bender that put a large dent in our new car, and after that, we got stuck in heavy Los Angeles traffic.

After sitting in the stop-and-go traffic for a long time, we pulled off the freeway to find a restroom. The area we were in looked sketchy, but we really had to go, so we pulled into a McDonald's. I used the restroom and then waited for my husband to come out of the men's room.

As I waited, I noticed a thirtysomething woman looking at me. When I made eye contact with her, she looked away. Over the next few minutes, I noticed her glancing at me several more times before she walked over to me.

"Excuse me," she said. "I'm really down on my luck right now, and I'm wondering if you could spare a dollar to help me out."

"Let me see," I said as I pulled out my wallet. I only had a twenty-dollar bill, so I told her, "Oh, I'm sorry, I don't."

She looked deflated but thanked me for checking anyway.

As she walked away, I thought about how I hadn't even known that I had twenty dollars because it wasn't important to me. It's not that I'm rich, but I'm financially comfortable enough that I don't have to keep a careful tab of how much money I spend from day to day. Then I thought about how one dollar was important enough to this woman to push her to ask a stranger for help.

"Wait," I called to her. "Why don't you take this?"

As I handed her the twenty, I could see the surprise on her face and then a look of deep gratitude as she thanked me profusely. I knew that I had made her day—perhaps even her week.

And she had made my day or week too, as the incident boosted my mood considerably.

CHAPTER 8

Practice Loving-Kindness

*May all beings, omitting none, feel safe and content
and happy, and live with ease.*

—The Metta Sutta

One day last spring I woke up with a raging sinus headache and felt crabby. When Paul wished me a cheerful "Good morning, sweetie," I grunted a surly "Morning" before I launched into complaining about my headache, my allergies, the fact that the bathroom sink was clogged again, and a list of other frustrations. My prognosis for the day was grim.

As I showered, I began to silently repeat the phrase *May I be happy* over and over. *May I be happy. May I be happy.* I continued this practice throughout my morning routine and found that it distracted me, at least a bit, from my headache and bummer mood.

Then while I was preparing my morning oatmeal, I pictured Paul in my mind and mentally sent him the wish *May you be happy.* I silently sent this wish over and over: *May you be happy, Paul. May you be happy.*

After sending Paul these secret wishes for a while, I scribbled, *Sorry for being crabby, I love you* on a bright pink sticky note. I quickly slipped the message under the bathroom door while Paul was showering.

When Paul got out of the shower, he came over to me and gave me a heartfelt hug. Then he looked me in the eye and said, "You're wonderful." He said this with a lot of feeling, and it made me feel really good.

After this I drove to a local coffee shop to do some writing. After writing for an hour or so, I took a break and began silently sending the wish *May you be happy* to the stylish thirtysomething woman sitting across the table from me. *May you be happy, stylish lady, may you be happy.* I next mentally sent the same wish to the pretty goth-styled barista, then to a group of older ladies engrossed in conversation, and then to everyone else in the shop, one at a time.

After sending secret loving wishes to everyone in the coffee shop, I felt moved to do something else kind, so I wrote, *Hi! May you be happy* ☺, on two sheets of paper. I handed one note to the group of older ladies, who read it, laughed, and thanked me, and then I handed the second note to the stylish woman, who thanked me even before she read the note.

After this, I went to the bathroom. When I came out, the stylish woman approached me and said, "I have to tell you that I notice energy in people, and when I saw you sitting in the shop, I immediately felt your good energy. So when you handed me that paper, I said 'thank you' before I even read it because I knew if you were giving me something, it would be good!"

On hearing this, my hands flew to my heart. "I'm so

touched," I said tearfully. She wrapped her arms around me, and I hugged her back. We exchanged a few more words and hugged again, and then I walked out of the coffee shop on cloud nine.

I felt so happy after this that I couldn't believe I'd woken up on the wrong side of the bed that morning.

⌣

My habit of silently wishing myself and others well may sound strange, but this practice, called *loving-kindness*, has been done for more than two thousand years as a way to develop an inner friendliness for yourself and others. It does this by shedding light on our own innate goodness. Kindness and compassion are qualities we all have. Loving-kindness nurtures these qualities by helping us let go of mental habits of meanness and judgment. This practice also helps you cultivate greater happiness (more on this later).

A simple way to explain loving-kindness practice is that you silently send goodwill or loving wishes to yourself and others with the intention of generating feelings of care. For example, you might mentally send the wish *May you be happy* to each person you encounter while you're on your morning dog walk.

Of course there's more to it than that, and Louis and I will explain the nuances of this practice in a moment. But first we're excited to share research that suggests that loving-kindness does far more than just encourage you to be kind to others. It's also been shown to offer numerous benefits for you!

For example, in a study by Douglas Gentile and associates from Iowa State University, students were asked to walk around a building on campus for twelve minutes while looking at each person they encountered and thinking, *I wish for this person to be happy.*[76] The researchers found that the walkers who practiced sending loving-kindness reaped many more benefits than those in a control condition, including:

- Decreased anxiety
- Greater happiness
- Greater empathy
- Higher feelings of caring and connectedness

Numerous other studies have found these same benefits, and more. Research suggests that loving-kindness practice has tremendous positive effects, from increased positive emotions[77] to slowed aging. Other specific benefits of loving-kindness practice suggested by study findings include:

- Decreased episodes of depression and PTSD[78]
- Decreased number of migraines[79]
- Decrease in chronic pain[80]
- Decreased bias toward others[81]
- Curbed self-criticism[82]

So, Louis and I have to ask, With the simplicity of this practice and science finding all these benefits, is there any reason *not* to try it?

Basic Instruction for Loving-Kindness Practice

Loving-kindness involves silently sending goodwill wishes (e.g., *May you be happy*) to yourself and others. There are two ways to do this. One way is *informal loving-kindness practice*, which involves sending loving wishes to people you see as you go about your day. While waiting for everyone to arrive at your next Zoom meeting, for example, silently send the first person you see the wish *May you be happy*. Then mentally send the same wish to the next person on your computer screen, and then the next person, and so on. You can send silent loving wishes like this to anyone, such as your family members, friends, work colleagues, people you pass while walking down the street, customers you see in the shops, and even your pets and other animals.

Also make sure to send silent loving wishes to yourself! This is not self-centered or selfish, because if your mind is filled with self-judgment and self-hate, it's hard to be kind to yourself or anyone else.

See too if you can do the informal loving-kindness practice *without discrimination*. That means to send loving wishes not only to those you care about but also to people you don't know well (such as gas station attendants or neighbors you see only in passing) and even to people who cause an adverse reaction in you (such as a coworker who annoys you or a family member you're not getting along with).

The second method of practice is *loving-kindness meditation*. You do this by sitting with your eyes closed, bringing someone to mind, such as a loved one, and then silently directing loving wishes toward her. After sending this person loving wishes, you bring another person to mind and then send her loving wishes, and then do the same with another person, and so on. Loving-kindness meditation traditionally involves directing loving wishes to the following groups:

- A loved one
- Yourself
- A neutral person (such as a grocery store clerk or a neighbor you've never met)

- A difficult person (such as someone you find challenging, perhaps a grumpy family member or a
frustrating coworker)
- All beings everywhere

For both types of loving-kindness practice, it is important to note that you don't have to force feelings of care. If you don't feel loving while sending loving wishes, that's okay. You can think of sending goodwill wishes like planting seeds in your mind. The seeds will bear fruit in their own time. Your job is simply to plant the seeds and allow nature to take its course.

You should also feel free to choose loving wishes that feel right to *you*. As an example, it can be powerful to choose a wish that has personal meaning for you. You can also tailor the wishes you send to what you or another may need at the specific time. If you are feeling worried about something, for example, you might silently send yourself a wish such as *May I be free from worry* or *May I be peaceful*. The following list offers some ideas for phrases, or you may want to come up with your own:

- May you smile and enjoy this moment.
- May I stay strong.
- May you feel joy.
- May I know my worth.
- May you feel like you belong.
- May you live a life you love.
- May I remember my goodness.
- May you be peaceful.
- May you feel safe.
- May I be playful.
- May the world be kind to you.

Play around with the words until you decide what works best for you. Don't limit yourself!

Oh, and one last thing. Louis and I have a loving-kindness wish we want to send to you: *May you recognize that you are amazing just the way you are.*

Exercises

Exercise #1: Wish others well throughout the day.

This week, practice silently sending goodwill wishes to your family members, friends, coworkers, and others you encounter daily. Come up with a wish (i.e., *May you be happy*) to silently send to whomever you see. You'll find ample opportunities, such as when you're standing in line at a grocery store, walking down the street, attending a meeting, working out at the gym, standing in a crowd of people, sitting in a waiting room, and so on. Make sure to send loving wishes to yourself too.

Exercise #2: Tap into the force of self-love.

This week try a self-love meditation to help you cultivate deep feelings of care and friendliness for yourself.

1. Begin by getting in a comfortable position, either sitting or lying down. Let your eyes gently close. As best you can, recall a time when you were kind, generous, or caring.

2. As these memories and feelings emerge, mentally wish yourself the following, changing the phrases if you wish:
    - May I be kind to myself.
    - May I be peaceful.
    - May I be happy.
    - May I smile and enjoy this moment."

3. Continue reciting the phrases slowly for as long as you like. If feelings of unworthiness come up, breathe gently and accept that these feelings have arisen. Then remember your wish to be happy, and return to your phrases.

Exercise #3: Befriend the difficult.

Difficult emotions are a normal part of being human. In fact, in order to experience happiness, we first need to allow ourselves to experience *all* painful emotions. Loving-kindness can help you gently face difficult emotions with kindness, just as you would gently care for a loved one who is going through a rough time.

The next time you feel frustrated, angry, anxious, impatient, or judgmental with yourself, try sending yourself these loving wishes, changing the phrases if you wish:
- May I be filled with loving-kindness.
- May I be free from pain and sorrow.
- May I feel peace.

If you're feeling upset with someone else, you can also direct the loving wishes toward this person.

- May you be filled with loving-kindness.
- May you be free from pain and sorrow.
- May you feel peace.

Exercise #4: Extend loving-kindness toward all.

When you practice this meditation, you will be directing loving wishes to one or more of the following groups:

- A loved one
- Yourself
- A neutral person
- A difficult person
- All beings everywhere

The first time you do this practice, you may want to start by sending wishes to a loved one only and then gradually add groups of people over time.

1. Begin by getting in a comfortable position, either sitting or lying down. Let your eyes gently close. Now bring to mind someone who naturally makes you smile. This loved one could be your child, a relative you adore, your dog or cat, or anyone who naturally fills your heart with joy.

2. As much as you can, fill yourself up with love and
   care for this being while mentally wishing them
   the following, changing the phrases if you wish:
   - May you be happy.
   - May you be well.
   - May you be peaceful.

   Continue reciting the phrases for a moment
   while you are holding this person in your heart.

3. Now shift your attention to yourself. As best
   you can, recall your own good qualities, perhaps remembering a time when you did something kind for someone. Now mentally wish
   yourself the following:
   - May I be happy.
   - May I be well.
   - May I be peaceful.

   If feelings of unworthiness come up, breathe
   gently and accept that these feelings have
   arisen. Then remember your wish to be happy,
   and return to your phrases.

4. Now, if you wish, you can open your heart
   further and send goodwill wishes to a neutral
   person and then a difficult person, in the same
   manner.

5. Finally, conclude by offering loving-kindness to
   all beings everywhere.

CELESTE'S JOURNAL ENTRY: Loving-Kindness at a Rest Stop

While we were driving to San Diego to visit my sister, Paul pulled into a rest area so we could use the restroom. I got into the long bathroom line for the women's room; the wait was frustrating. After a few minutes it dawned on me that as I waited, I was judging the people around me . . .

I can't believe the woman ahead of me is wearing a black bra with a white see-through blouse. So tacky. And look, that other lady is coming out of the stall in this crappy rest area in a pair of stilettos? Come on! That's ridiculous.

I also noticed that I was judging myself . . .

Damn, I wish I had a body like hers! That woman over at the sink looks so cute and stylish; I wish I could look that good while traveling.

My first reaction to recognizing my judgments was to judge myself for being so judgmental. Then I remembered that one of the things I'd learned from my mindfulness practice was *not* to judge myself for being judgmental.

At this point I recognized that this was a perfect opportunity to practice loving-kindness. I reminded myself that everyone here wanted to be happy, just as I wanted to be happy. *Why not send them some encouragement?*

I silently sent the woman with the black bra ahead of me the wish *May you be happy.* Then I sent the same wish to the cute, stylish woman, the woman in the stilettos, and everyone else in line. I did this person by person, one at a time. Then I remembered to send myself some loving wishes too.

After a moment or so of sending loving wishes, I noticed that my body had softened; the tension I had been experiencing was gone! I felt less anxious about getting through the line and on to the next part of my day. I also felt less judgmental about others and myself.

Maybe it was all in my mind—but I felt that others now perceived me differently too. One woman made focused eye contact with me and smiled. I felt like she was silently communicating, *I feel your acceptance and love for me.* It was a micro-moment of connection—and it felt good.

CHAPTER 9

Open Your Heart to Suffering

*The less you open your heart to others,
the more your heart suffers.*

—Deepak Chopra

In early 2020 when Australia was fighting one of its worst-ever bushfire seasons and the media was repeatedly showing images of animals with singed fur, raw patches of burnt flesh, and blistered paws, Gray, a twentysomething American man, spoke up in an anxiety support group he attended about wanting to help in some way. The group decided to raise money to donate to the cause, and the group's moderator said she would match whatever they raised. They were able to raise a sizeable amount of money, which the group donated to the Australian Red Cross.

You have two choices when you see suffering:

- You can open your heart.
- You can pull a protective "shield" over your vulnerable center.

Only one choice is kind. And only one choice heals.

When We Open, We Heal

Opening your heart to the suffering of others gives you the opportunity to respond with compassion and kindness. But it's also the best healing you can give to yourself. Much of our unhappiness in life stems from being too "me-centered." When our thoughts are mostly centered on ourselves, we're bound to feel overwhelmed by our problems and challenges. Our focus narrows; we think about "me, me, me" and our unhappiness or pain. But if we open our hearts to the suffering of others— which may well be far worse than our own suffering—it takes our mind off our own struggles.

To cite a personal example, I spent weeks anxious and frustrated about my own concerns when the world was in crisis from the coronavirus pandemic. I worried about my finances, was annoyed when I couldn't find toilet paper and other basic grocery items, felt sad that I couldn't see people I cared about, and was frustrated about not being able to go out for dinner or to a coffee shop. My worries put me in a bummer mood much of the time.

Then one day I read on Facebook that a positive psychology leader I admired, Emiliya Zhivotovskaya, had lost her father to the coronavirus. As I thought about the suffering her father had to endure and the grief Emiliya and her family were dealing with, my heart opened to them, and my own suffering felt dramatically minimized.

Opening our heart is something that we often do naturally. But more often than we may realize, *we don't open our heart to others*. When we're busy, stressed, or dealing with our own suffering, for example, we may simply tune out or miss the suffering of others—even of those we love.

Also, if we happen to perceive another person as "less than" us or as "bad," it can close our heart to them and prevent us from seeing that they suffer, just like we do. This is something we all do at times (often unconsciously), especially with those who are different from us, which helps make the world divisive. Some of us feel this way, whether intentionally or unintentionally, about those who have different political or religious views from ours, or those who are of a different race, weight, age, gender, or class. My mom once posted something political on Facebook, for example, and a friend shot back a hateful response. She posted that my mom was "a disgrace" and said other derogatory things about her. Viewing my mom as different had closed this woman's heart and caused her to be abusive.

Sometimes we don't have the opportunity to open our heart because others' suffering is concealed in some way. For example, if you're a Facebook user and you scroll through your feed, you might imagine that everyone else you know who is on Facebook is living a happy, exciting, friend-and-family-filled life. But this may not be true! The reality is that most people don't broadcast their struggles on Facebook, so you don't see or read about them. With the exception of those closest to you, it's also uncommon for your coworkers, classmates, and others you interact with daily to share when they're struggling.

Even someone who appears to have it all together may be suffering immensely. I remember being astounded in 2014 when TV personality Wayne Brady revealed his battle with debilitating depression. I had been watching Brady for years on the improvisational comedy show *Whose Line Is It Anyway?* and was impressed with his quick wit, humor, and lovely singing voice. I often imagined (with a little envy) how blissful he must be in his problem-free existence as a popular TV personality. The news that he suffers from depression was a stark reminder that we often don't see the struggles others are going through.

Finally, we often close our hearts to suffering to avoid feeling uncomfortable (something you'll learn how to counteract in this chapter). Consider your likely interactions with a homeless person: Do you make eye contact and offer a smile or a dollar, or do you retrain your eyes elsewhere and cross the street to avoid a potential interaction or exchange? Or what if someone you love or like is ill, perhaps with cancer or Alzheimer's disease: Do you call to see if you can help in any way, such as by picking up some groceries for them, or do you avoid calling because you don't know what to say or because it hurts to see someone you care about in pain? While I'm not proud of it, some years ago I began avoiding a coworker after she told me she had cancer because I no longer knew what to say to her; today I truly hope I would choose differently if confronted with a similar situation.

Since it can be easy to close our hearts, here are three simple methods for opening your heart to the suffering of others:
1. Notice suffering.
2. Send a silent loving wish to them.
3. Silence your "inner fixer."

Notice Suffering

My sister, Michelle, is generally good at showing up for things we plan to do, but there was a period of several months when she canceled on me numerous times at the last minute. I finally confronted her about this trend, only to discover that the cause of her uncharacteristic behavior was intense distress over some serious relationship problems. Her unusual behavior was a clue that she was suffering, but I didn't realize the significance behind her actions.

You can't open your heart to suffering you're not aware of. That's why noticing unusual behavior patterns in others and considering potential causes is an important pathway for opening your heart. People who are suffering "often offer clues," write researchers Monica Worline and Jane Dutton in *Awakening Compassion at Work*. "Sometime[s] they are not as engaged as usual. Sometimes their bodies convey exhaustion or tension. Sometimes their facial expressions display sadness or anger."[83] Whenever someone is acting out of character, this is a clue that they may be suffering.

One of the most challenging as well as the most rewarding times to notice clues is when someone is being unkind to you. Most of us get too caught up in our own hurt or anger to recognize that the other person is suffering too. But they *are* suffering. In fact, being unkind is a blatant clue that someone is suffering immensely and doesn't know how to handle their pain. Responding back in kind will only add to the suffering you both feel, so if you can perceive unkindness as a clue that someone may be suffering, it can open your heart to responding with compassion.

A Balanced Approach to Noticing Suffering

It's important to be *balanced* about how much suffering you notice because it's possible to be overwhelmed by it—which may cause you to check out. This may happen, for example, if we consume too much news. And that's easy to do these days. Negative and upsetting news crops up on our phones and laptops. We receive, read, and hear "emergency" alerts. We come across a horrible headline or hate-filled comment on social media. We see a billboard or Amber Alert about an upsetting incident.

It's difficult to escape from the many news outlets today, and constantly viewing sensationalized negative news and pictures of violent crime, disaster, and heartache can actually numb us to suffering. It may make us feel helpless and hopeless, which can clench our heart shut and make us close down to others. However, it's important to note that Louis and I are not saying you should be uninformed but rather that you consume news *mindfully*. Consider whether the amount of news you consume is opening your heart—or closing it. Then adjust your consumption appropriately if need be.

Send a Silent Loving Wish

Even if you are careful about how much news you consume, it is sometimes hard not to feel overwhelmed by the suffering you see around you. For example, let's imagine you turn on the news and learn that a school shooting near you killed a six-year-old boy. One way to counteract the fear and helplessness this news creates is to switch from feeling empathy to feeling compassion.

Many people confuse empathy and compassion, but they are different. *Empathy* means actually feeling the pain of others; *compassion* means feeling warmth, concern, and care for another. Research suggests that too much empathy can be distressing and prevent you from having the cognitive and emotional resources to help another.[84] On the other hand, experiencing compassion can override feelings of distress and lead to well-being for you and greater availability to others.

A simple way to make the switch from empathy to compassion is to send a silent loving wish, such as *I wish for you to be happy and free from suffering*, whenever you see someone in distress. This may be done with suffering you see either in real life or on the news. When my husband is in a bad mood, for example, I sometimes silently send him the wish *May you feel happy and calm* over and over. I find that it often protects me from catching his mood and responding negatively—and sometimes it boosts his mood too!

Silence Your "Inner Fixer"

In *How to Listen So People Will Talk*, author and speaker Becky Harling writes, "Many of us wrestle with a fix-it mentality. A friend or spouse confides in us, and we've got just the creative solution. We know exactly what to do."[85] Unfortunately, this approach often doesn't help. Have you ever had an issue and you're very upset, and someone listens to you for a minute and then says, "Why don't you do this . . . ?" How does this feel to you?

I remember confiding to Rick—a guy I was dating in my twenties—about how frustrated I was that I was having trouble losing weight. His response? "That's easy; all you have to do is eat less." Not the response I was hoping for.

Sure, we mean well when we want to fix things for someone:

we don't want others, especially those we care about, to suffer. When we dive in to "fix," however, the other person often feels like we don't get how depressed, hurt, or angry they feel. They don't feel *understood*. What's more, our unsolicited advice often comes across as judgmental and condescending. It implies that we don't believe the other person has the ability to solve their own problem. Most problems are complex, and it's impossible to know every detail of the problem the person is facing. So if we try to solve someone else's problem in a few minutes, we can be perceived as demeaning them.

When you're with someone who is suffering, "rather than asserting yourself as the one with the answer," suggests Harling, "position yourself as a friend who is seeking to understand."[86] Do this by listening carefully and then validating them by saying, "That sounds hard. I can see how this is really bothering you." Or "Wow, you sound upset, that really got you going." Then get more information. "Tell me more."

Understand them and empathize with how they are feeling. This is what they really want and need in this moment.

Exercises

Exercise #1: Look for clues.

Set an intention to notice suffering this week. In everyone you see and interact with, make it a point to look for "clues," such as someone acting out of character, not being as engaged or sensitive as usual, or appearing exhausted, tense, sad, irritable, and/or angry.

So, for example, when your partner snaps at you, see this as a clue that suffering may be below the irritability. Or when a shop clerk is rude to you, see this as a clue that suffering may be below their insensitive behavior.

Exercise #2: Send a loving wish.

Whenever you become aware of suffering this week, mentally send those who are suffering the loving wish *May you be happy and free from suffering.* See if you can hold the suffering person in your heart and mind for a minute or two while reciting this phrase.

Exercise #3: Silence your "inner fixer."

When you're with someone who is suffering this week, see if you can silence your inner fixer. Instead of trying to fix their problem or make their pain go away, seek to understand what they are going through. Do this by listening carefully to them and then validating them with a statement that shows you understand, such as: "That sounds hard. I can see how this is really bothering you." Then get more information by asking them to share more about what they're dealing with.

CELESTE'S JOURNAL ENTRY: The Grumpy Barista

Paul and I went to a coffee shop one morning for a latte. As we approached the counter, an older female clerk with a thick gray ponytail, numerous visible tattoos, extremely dark eye shadow, and a face that looked like it had seen a lot of pain glumly asked, "How are you?"

"I'm great," I said brightly. "How are you?"

"Still here," she snarled.

Why would this shop hire such a grumpy employee? I wondered. *She can't be good for business.*

Then I remembered what I'd read in a book by the Buddhist monk Thich Nhat Hanh about looking deeper at people who are unkind. It dawned on me that this woman's demeanor was a sign that she was suffering deeply. I wondered what horrors in her life had caused her face to look so pained.

As I pondered this, my heart opened to her. I wanted to do something kind for her, something that would make her feel better, but I wasn't sure what to do. After ordering my drink, I sat down at a table near her and began silently sending her loving wishes like:

May you be happy.

May you, coffee shop lady, be free from suffering.

May you feel peace.

As I repeated these phrases over and over, my heart swelled with compassion for her. At the same time, I felt disappointed. I felt like what I was doing wasn't enough. It wasn't going to make her life, or even her day, better.

When I thought more about this incident later, however, I realized that I *had* made a difference. Had I not recognized this woman's suffering, I would have been caught up in judging her. This would have had me complaining to my husband about how unfriendly this clerk was, likely over and over again! This would have put both my husband and me into a bummer mood. And moods are contagious, so that's what he and I would have been spreading for the rest of the day. I realized that *opening my heart to the suffering of others always matters*. If I can do this more often, I can make a difference in the lives of those around me and in my own life. If lots of people did this more often, it would make an enormous difference. It might even change the world!

CHAPTER 10

Do Random Acts of Kindness

Together we can change the world just one random act of kindness at a time.

—Ron Hall

Jenny spent a lot of time walking in her neighborhood, careful to stay six feet apart from others, while sheltering in place during the coronavirus pandemic. One day she smiled and waved across the street at a middle-aged woman with a thick blonde ponytail. The woman smiled back, and then Jenny asked her if she was doing okay with supplies like toilet paper. The woman shouted back, "I can't find any flour!"

"Have you tried Albertsons? They had it the last time I was there," Jenny suggested.

"I'm too afraid to go to the store," the woman answered. "I care for my elderly mother, and I know she won't make it if she gets the virus, so I'm trying to be very careful."

"I have flour," Jenny said, "and I live just around the corner.

My name is Jenny. Why don't you follow me to my house and I'll get some for you?"

After some hesitation, the woman agreed and seemed very grateful for the kindness. It made Jenny feel good to help the woman out as well.

Some weeks later, while Jenny was out for her usual walk, she heard someone behind her call out, "Are you Jenny?"

"Yes!" Jenny responded while turning around to face the person.

"I'm Joanna, the woman you gave the flour to, and I just wanted to thank you again. I've been telling everyone about what you did for me. I just really wanted you to know how much I appreciated what you did."

Until the woman reminded her, Jenny had forgotten about giving the woman the flour, and she was amazed at how much of an impact this small kindness had made. Listening to the woman's heartfelt thank-you boosted Jenny's mood for the rest of the day. It also prompted her to purposefully look for random ways to be kind as the pandemic continued. Doing so gave her a sense of purpose and helped her stay remarkably positive through her own challenges with this crisis.

A *random act of kindness* (RAK) is simply a small or large unexpected act of charity or helpfulness. The phrase was coined in 1982 when writer Anne Herbert wrote, "Practice random kindness and senseless acts of beauty" on a placemat. From there the phrase spread, slowly at first but with growing momentum. Then in 1993 Herbert published the book *Random Kindness and Senseless Acts of Beauty*, and people everywhere began doing random kindnesses, such as giving up that good parking spot that's "rightfully" yours to another car, leaving a generous tip for your waitress, sending a handwritten letter to someone you care about, and raking leaves for a neighbor unasked. People sometimes use the term to refer to acts performed for strangers, but the acts can also be done for friends, family, animals, and the earth.

While random acts of kindness are intended to benefit the people receiving them, research suggests that the people doing the random good deeds also feel pleasure and happiness as a result (in much the same way you and I derive pleasure from performing planned or intentional acts of kindness, as has been detailed earlier in the book). The results of one study revealed that eighty-three students who performed random kind acts for an hour and a half experienced greater happiness, among other benefits.[87]

In fact, in his book *Flourish*, psychologist Martin Seligman shares, "We scientists have found that doing a kindness produces the single most reliable momentary increase in well-being of any exercise we have tested."[88] In addition to what he's learned from research, Seligman has personally experienced the mood boost from a RAK. In *Flourish*, he tells the story of waiting forty-five minutes in a slow-moving post office line created by a one-penny stamp increase. When he finally made it to the front, he bought ten sheets of one-cent stamps and then shouted, "Who needs one-penny stamps? They're free!" The crowd burst into applause as they clustered around him to receive his gifts and escape the wait in line. This incident took two minutes and cost Seligman a mere ten dollars, yet he shares that "it was one of the most satisfying moments of my life."[89]

There are many random acts of kindness you can do. Here are some ideas to get you started.

21 Random Acts of Kindness You Could Do Today

1. **Give a sincere compliment.** Compliments can be powerful. My sister, Michelle, shared that when she was a freshman at Cal State University in Stanislaus, she was shy and didn't want to look at people in the eyes because she felt so insecure. Then she met fellow student Emerson, and one day he told her, "You know, you have a really nice smile. You should show it off." His encouragement gave her the confidence to begin looking at people and smiling. When she started doing this, her confidence grew and she began making more friends—her life improved and blossomed! Michelle believes that this one small compliment transformed her life profoundly.

2. **Smile, say hello, have a chat, give a few dollars, or buy a meal for a homeless person.** Or do what Orly Wahba suggests in her book *Kindness Boomerang*: "Buy a dozen sandwiches and pass them out to homeless folks in a busy area."[90]

3. **Express a heartfelt thank-you.** Recently while Paul and I were eating dinner, Paul asked me about my day. After I shared details about my mundane afternoon of chores (grocery shopping, cleaning the bathrooms, and the like), Paul looked at me and said, "I know I don't say it enough, but I really appreciate all that you do." I could tell he meant what he was saying, and this touched me deeply. It made me feel appreciated. (In fact, I'm still glowing over this comment right now as I write this!)

4. **Look to include others, especially those who are forgotten or who are in need of understanding or help.** Stephen, my dog walker, often attends music

festivals. These events are so large that it's common for people to search for the friends they're supposed to meet and yet never find them. Stephen and his friends now are in the habit of keeping an eye out for people in this situation and upon finding them, asking if they need help or if they want to hang out with them for the day since they're all alone.

5. **Write a gratitude letter.** If someone did something for you that you are extremely grateful for but you never expressed your deep appreciation, write a letter telling this person why you are grateful to them and how their behavior affected your life. Last year my friend Joanna's husband listed all the reasons he was grateful for her on one page, framed it, and gave it to her for her birthday. She was incredibly touched by this gesture and couldn't thank her husband enough—even though he was the one thanking her!

6. **Do a five-minute favor.** In his bestselling book *Give and Take: Why Helping Others Drives Our Success,* Wharton University professor Adam Grant suggests carving out just five minutes of your day to do something that will benefit the lives of others—without expecting anything in return. You might, for example, introduce individuals who might benefit from knowing each other, call your mom, or write a thank-you note.

7. **Hold the door open for someone.** Holding the door open is a thoughtful act you can easily do for others every day. My mom, who walks with a cane, tells me that she really appreciates when others hold the door open for her because she often finds it hard to open doors while holding her cane.

8. **Do an act of kindness for the environment.** There are many simple ways you can help the earth, such as picking up litter you see while out for a walk, saying no to a store bag for carriable items, planting a tree, walking or biking to work, or cutting your shower short to save water. When I walk my dog in the neighboring town of San Clemente, I often see a middle-aged woman walking a small dog and picking up litter, which she places in a large trash bag she brings with her. I struck up a conversation with her once, and she told me that she picks up litter while walking her dog twice every day.

9. **Leave a pretty potted plant on someone's doorstep.** When I returned from a recent trip, I was surprised (and delighted) to find that my neighbor Anna had left me a beautiful orchid on my front porch.

10. **Write inspirational sticky notes.** Carry a stack of sticky notes in your purse or pocket, and write positive statements on them such as *Psst . . . you're awesome*, *You are beautiful inside and out*, and *Hey, you're great!* Then leave them anywhere that they'll brighten someone else's day, like around an office, at a bus stop, in your kiddo's lunch, on a parked car—or on your partner's bathroom mirror.

11. **Talk to someone who seems uncomfortable or lonely.** The next time you are at a party or gathering, search out someone who is alone or looks uncomfortable and initiate a conversation. This will take the burden off this person and will oftentimes make them feel relieved and grateful.

12. **Show kindness to animals.** Look for opportunities to share some kindness with an animal, such as taking

your pooch for an extra-long walk, putting a birdhouse in your yard, choosing a meat-free lunch, spoiling your dog or cat with homemade treats, or resisting the urge to squash a spider. A few years ago, Paul and I started capturing the spiders we found in our home so that we could release them outside. It is surprising how good it makes us feel to do this.

13. **Share a kindness story.** If someone has been kind to you or if you heard or saw someone doing a good deed, share it with others. Hearing stories of kindness reminds people that while bad things happen, good things happen a lot too! This instills hope. What's more, since hearing about a good deed prompts others to act in kind, you'll be perpetuating a cascade of ever-increasing happiness.

14. **Show off your child's art.** When you display your child's artwork, you are showing your child support. You might share their artwork on Facebook, frame and hang up several pieces in your home, or create a picture book with their art. Or you can hold an art exhibition by displaying select pieces of your child's art in your home or backyard and invite friends and relatives to come view it. When I was young, my mom held an art exhibition for my siblings and me in our backyard that made me feel seen, valued, and loved.

15. **Offer change when the person in front of you at the register comes up short.** Elizabeth Zack, one of this book's editors, shared that while reading this book, she was inspired to give two pennies to the lady ahead of her in line at the store one day so that the cashier didn't have to break bills and count additional change. This made her feel good—and it was just two cents!

16. **Write a positive review.** If you have a positive experience with a company or product, write a review as a way to thank the company for doing a good job and to help others have this same enjoyable experience as well. When I read the book *14 Steps to Self-Publishing a Book* by Mike Kowis, I found it very helpful, so I wrote a positive review on Amazon to help other authors discover and benefit from this book too.

17. **Host a pink flamingo potluck in your neighborhood.** I read about this kindness idea in writer and podcaster Nicole J. Phillips's book *The Negativity Remedy: Unlocking More Joy, Less Stress, and Better Relationships through Kindness* and thought it sounded fun. Here's how you do it: "Send out a flyer to the people on your block and tell them they are invited to your pink flamingo party. They will get a reminder the morning of the party on their way to work because you will put up pink flamingos in your yard early on this day."

18. **Take a child on a date.** Plan a special outing, such as going to a park, the zoo, or a movie, with your child or with a niece or nephew. This kind of special attention from an adult can make a child feel loved and valued. While I was growing up, my parents took turns taking my five siblings and me on one-on-one outings every so often. These outings, like when I went ice skating with my dad and to see the movie *Grease* with my mom, are among my happiest childhood memories.

19. **Tell someone that you believe in them.** On her first tournament of her first year playing college intramural racquetball, my friend Laura competed in the lowest division and scored dead last. This was a blow to her

already low self-esteem and she thought about quitting, but then her coach commented to her, "Laura, do you know you're a diamond in the rough?" She took these words to heart and worked hard so that by the next year, she was competing in the highest division and winning matches!

20. **Send someone a book, just because.** If you come across a book you think someone would enjoy, send them a copy. Over the past few years, I've become virtual friends with the host of the *Positive Psychology Podcast*, Kristen Truempy. One day, out of the blue, I received the book *The Happiness Passport* by Megan C. Hayes from Kristen. It wasn't even my birthday; she simply sent it because she thought I'd appreciate it. I was deeply touched by this kindness and will never forget it.

21. **Send a handwritten note.** There's something about a handwritten note arriving in the mail that just feels more meaningful than a text or an email. One day while writing this book, I received a handwritten letter from my mother-in-law, Rose, that said the following:

Good morning Sunshine,

"Let no one come to you without leaving better and happier. Be the loving expression of God's kindness: kindness in your face, kindness in your eyes, kindness in your smile." —Mother Teresa

Have a great day!!

Peace, joy, hope and love

P.S. Thank you for your caring and loving spirit.

This card touched my heart deeply. It made me feel loved, cared for, and appreciated. I wanted to pay this kindness forward, so I sent similar notes to several people I care about.

Seek out an opportunity to cheer someone up every day. Send a note to a long-lost friend, play a game with a child, hold open a door, buy coffee for the person behind you in line, and tell your neighbor that her new haircut looks absolutely fabulous.

The world would be a different place if we all practiced daily random acts of kindness. Here are some exercises to help you change the world one random act of kindness at a time.

Exercises

Exercise #1: Do five random acts of kindness this week.

Be on the lookout for opportunities to do wholly unexpected kind actions this week—and just do them!

Exercise #2: Do "extra" kind acts for someone you love.

Think of a relationship that is important to you. It could be with your spouse, a parent, your child, or a close friend. Practice doing random acts of kindness specifically for this person this week. These should be over and above kind acts that you typically do for them.

Exercise #3: Do random acts of kindness for someone who is struggling.

Try to think of a person you know who seems to be struggling or is in pain, or who is somehow isolated, and make it a point to do random acts of kindness for them this week.

Exercise #4: Do random acts of kindness for animals and/or the earth.

Animals and the earth need your love and kindness too! Look for ways to do random acts of kindness for your pet, wildlife, other animals, and/or the environment this week.

CELESTE'S JOURNAL ENTRY: An Unexpected Gift

I popped into a grocery store to pick up a few things. It had some beautiful flowering plants on sale for just $2.25. Thinking that it would be nice to brighten my front porch, I put a pot of bright yellow tulips into my cart.

As I was checking out, the young female clerk with vibrant red hair striped with pink streaks in the front gushed over my tulips. On a whim, I decided to give them to her and said, "They are for you."

Thinking that I was kidding, she laughed, so I repeated, "Seriously, I've just bought them for you."

We went back and forth several times before she realized I was serious. When this dawned on her, she gushed, "I think I'm gonna cry, that was so nice. Can I give you a hug?"

"Sure," I said, and we embraced.

I walked out of the store with a beaming smile and feeling happier than I'd felt in a long time.

CHAPTER 11

Meet Rudeness with Love

How people treat you is their karma,
how you react is yours.

—Wayne Dyer

Carol and her husband were walking their dog, Bella, in an upscale neighborhood, and Bella squatted to pee on someone's lawn. An older man backing his car out of the driveway began pounding his finger against his window to get Carol's attention. Then he rolled down his window and shouted, "Don't let your dog do that there! You shouldn't ruin other people's lawns like that. It's people like you who are turning this neighborhood into a ghetto."

Carol responded sincerely, "Oh, I'm sorry that bothered you. I'll make sure she doesn't go on your lawn again. It's so beautiful out today; I hope you enjoy your day."

"Okay, well, just don't let it happen again," the man responded.

"Of course," Carol promised. "It looks like you take great care of your yard, and I can understand why you don't want dogs doing their business on it."

"I do like to keep up my yard," the man responded, his demeanor noticeably softening. "It's the first thing people see when they come to visit, and I want it to look nice."

"Well, it shows."

Now beaming, the man responded brightly, "Thank you, I really appreciate that. I hope you have a lovely day."

"You, too."

As the man drove away, Carol's husband said, "That was amazing! You're like a grumpy old man whisperer or something!"

Carol's story is striking because most of us would make a different choice in that situation: we'd probably grumble something under our breath while quickly walking away, and then gripe to others about it and let it ruin our day—or at the very least stew about it for a while. Kindness is simply not the first impulse most of us have when someone gives us attitude, cuts us off in traffic, or snaps at us over something minor. They were rude, so why should *we* be kind to *them*?

One reason is that it's a way to be kind to yourself. Sounds like a paradox, right? However, here's a different way to think about it: "When our minds are full of anger and hatred toward others, in fact we are the ones who are actually suffering," says meditation teacher Sharon Salzberg.[91] When we respond with kindness to another's rudeness or obnoxious behavior, we can let go of our own painful mind state.

Another reason is that the rude behavior may be unintentional. Here's an example from my own life. Some years ago I'd invited a few friends to my house for dinner. I served a specialty pizza from a wonderful local pizza parlor. After dinner, one of my friends pulled me aside and said, "That wasn't very considerate of you to invite people to your house for a meal and serve take-out pizza." I was surprised this upset her as I couldn't imagine that somebody could be offended by that . . . and therein lies the problem! Christine Porath, an associate professor at Georgetown University who studies the effects of incivility on people, explains that rudeness "is in the eyes of the recipient."[92] What you consider rude may not be the same as what others consider rude, which means that a lot of rude behavior is unintentional.

Research also suggests that a kind response to rudeness has a strong potential to lead to positive outcomes for you as well as the offender—and even for others beyond the two of you! Before we get to this research, however, it's important to note that meeting rudeness with love does not mean tolerating abuse or letting someone walk all over you. This is *not* kind to you. Rather, it means respecting yourself while also being respectful of the other person. For example, a kind response when a waiter is rude to you might be to not take it personally (this is respectful to you) while also resisting the temptation to get even in some way (this is respectful to them).

Please also note that the exercises in this chapter are meant for dealing with day-to-day rude or "minor"—if we can call them such—unkind behaviors, like someone stealing our parking space or a coworker snapping at us. Being on the receiving end of inappropriate and unacceptable behaviors, such as any form of abuse or assault, are beyond the scope of this book; for help in dealing with such issues, consider seeking the advice of a medical, health, or other competent professional. Now let's look at the research. University of the Fraser Valley School of Business associate professor Kirsten Robertson did a study where she conducted interviews with service employees to determine what response styles avoided escalating an uncivil encounter. First, she found four types of responses employees typically give when responding to a rude customer:

1. **Reactive incivility**—raising voice, swearing, speaking condescendingly, and/or abruptly walking away

2. **Subversive incivility**—providing acceptable service but service deliberately below personal standards, and/ or providing "sarcastically good" service to spite rude customers

3. **Submissive civility**—apologizing without meaning it, and/or appearing nice on the surface to end the challenging interaction

4. **Resolute civility**—choosing not to let others' attitudes affect you, choosing to respond politely, trying to lighten mood, and/or proactively trying to solve customers' problems[93]

Of these styles, the resolute civility response style, which is basically sincere kindness, was found to have the strongest potential to lead to positive outcomes for both parties in the interaction. According to Robertson, this response style tended to:

- Deescalate the situation
- Calm the customer down
- Change the customer's attitude
- Transform a negative interaction into a positive one

- Lead to positive interpersonal consequences for service employees, such as feeling relieved, feeling proud because they believed they were doing the right thing despite the customer's behavior, and experiencing personal growth[94]

It is important to note that Robertson also found that insincere politeness (submissive civility), such as when service workers apologized without meaning it or appeared nice on the surface to end the challenging interaction, did not improve the situation and led them to feeling ashamed, devalued, and angry—and even to ruminate about seeking revenge. This means that faking kindness does us no good! For you and others to benefit, kindness has to be sincere.

Did you know that by choosing a kind response, you can even stop the spread of rudeness to others? A study from the University of Florida, for example, found that rude behavior is contagious.[95] In this study, ninety graduate students were followed for seven weeks as they conducted business negotiation exercises. During the seven weeks, they switched partners several times. Students who described their first negotiating partner as "rude" were more likely to behave rudely to someone else, thereby spreading rudeness like a disease!

By doing your best to stay polite and courteous, you may be able to stop a rudeness epidemic.

Incivility in the Workplace

It would be great if everyone treated us respectfully all the time, but unfortunately, this is not reality. In fact, Christine Porath's research has found that 98 percent of people report experiencing incivility, which is disrespect or rudeness, at work. This rudeness includes a lot of different behaviors, such as publicly mocking or belittling someone, teasing in ways that sting, or taking credit for wins while pointing the finger at others when difficulties arise.

The costs of such incivility are greater than we think: Christine's research suggests that people who are the targets of incivility at work experience negative reactions such as spending an inordinate amount of time worrying about incidents, decreased ability to pay attention, impaired creativity, and reduced productivity. Her research also suggests that once people are exposed to rudeness, they are *three times less likely* to help others, and their willingness to share drops by *more than half*.[96] What's more, those simply around incivility are more likely to have dysfunctional or aggressive thoughts.[97] If left unchecked, workplace incivility can damage your health, disrupt your relationships, and leave you feeling depressed, anxious, and burned out.

In her Tedx Talk "Why Being Respectful to Your Coworkers Is Good for Business," Porath shares:

"Incivility is a bug. It's contagious, and we become carriers of it just by being around it. And this isn't confined to the workplace. We can catch this virus anywhere—at home, online, in schools, and in our communities. It affects our emotions, our motivation, our performance, and how we treat others. It even affects our attention and can take some of our brainpower."[98]

Thankfully, in this chapter you'll learn ways to make you less likely to catch and spread this "bug."

How to Meet Rudeness with Love

Even if we recognize the benefits of meeting rudeness with love, it can be challenging to do. Our gut reaction is often to respond in kind or internalize it, causing us to think about it over and over again, robbing us of our peace of mind. So we need some tools in our tool kit to help us pause and respond differently. Here are four that Louis and I have found particularly helpful.

Tool #1: Soothe yourself

If someone mistreats you, often the kindest initial response you can make is to soothe yourself. Not only is this kind to you, but it also has a lot of power in helping you control your behavior. If you are really upset with someone, your brain starts pumping stress hormones to tighten muscles and prepare you to fight or flee. This is a good thing if a tiger is chasing you, but not a good thing if you are running a staff meeting and get angry at a rude coworker! If you can intervene and soothe your own pain, you will have a greater capacity to choose kindness.

One simple method to soothe your pain is what Dan Siegel, clinical professor at the UCLA School of Medicine, calls the "name it to tame it" approach. All you do is name the emotion you are feeling. For example, say mentally or aloud, "I am feeling angry," or "I have a tight ball of nerves in my gut." Research shows that when you do this, your brain will secrete soothing neurotransmitters that calm you down.[99] This sounds too good to be true, but I've found it really works.

Tool #2: Remember that there's always a "backstory"

When someone is unkind, they are usually suffering in some way. They may be having a bad day, week, or life. Or perhaps they are miserable in their marriage, fed up with their boss, or dealing with some other issue. My friend and spiritual teacher Jeanne Sanner puts it this way:

> There's always a backstory. We don't have to know what it is; we just have to remember it's there. We can see each other as coming from love or as wounded. Would you get angry at a wounded puppy that growls at you? You would have compassion for them. When someone is unkind, we can see it as a call for love.[100]

When we remember this, it helps us respond to rude behavior with kindness and compassion. In fact, an experience in a grocery store I had some years ago helps me remember this.

While I was pulling a head of romaine lettuce from an overstuffed shelf, three other heads fell to the floor. The fiftysomething female produce clerk standing near me scowled at me and then snapped at me with an attitude. My gut reaction was to snap right back, but I did not: I kept my mouth shut, but I left the produce aisle fuming. When I got to the checkout line, however, I realized that I forgot to get an avocado, so I had to return to the produce department. As I picked out an avocado, I overheard the woman who snapped at me sharing with a coworker how she thought she had made a mistake coming into work that day with her mom having passed away the day before. On hearing this, I immediately softened toward the clerk and her behavior.

Tool #3: Reframe rude behavior as an opportunity

Our response to rudeness is often so habitual that we react in the same hurtful ways over and over again without recognizing that we can choose an alternative response. But we can! In the research mentioned earlier in this chapter, Robertson found that service workers who responded with resolute civility shared that they were able to not let others' attitudes affect them and to respond with kindness because they perceived rude behavior not as a personal attack but as an opportunity for personal growth or a way to practice and expand their interpersonal skills.

Could a rude person be *a teacher in disguise?* They may be if you reframe your experience with them as an *opportunity*—an opportunity to practice being less judgmental, more understanding, less reactive, and more kind. Zen teacher Charlotte Joko Beck says:

> *"Life always gives us exactly the teacher we need*
> *at every moment. This includes every mosquito, every*
> *misfortune, every red light, every traffic jam, every*
> *obnoxious supervisor (or employee), every illness, every*
> *loss, every moment of joy or depression, every addiction,*
> *every piece of garbage, every breath."* [101]

Tool #4: Write about it

If you've been treated rudely, you probably know how hard it can be to get over it. We often replay uncivil encounters over and over in our minds after the event. Not only does this prevent us from putting the event behind us, but this can also be a blow to our self-esteem and trigger feelings of insecurity and helplessness. One way to help you process your feelings and bring closure is to write about the experience. Research suggests that writing about an extremely stressful event can create significant healing. In fact, one study found that participants who wrote about their most traumatic experiences for fifteen minutes four days in a row experienced better health outcomes up to four months later.[102]

Meeting rudeness with kindness helps us be kind to ourselves and others, stops the spread of rude behavior, and presents us with an opportunity for growth. The following exercises offer practical ways to cope with rudeness by putting kindness into action.

Exercises

Exercise #1: Soothe yourself.

If you become really upset by someone's behavior this week, make it a point to soothe yourself. In the moment when you feel your anger rising, try using the "name it to tame it" approach. To do this, simply name what you are feeling. For example, say to yourself mentally or aloud, "I am feeling angry."

Exercise #2: Remind yourself that there's always a backstory.

Whenever someone is rude to you this week, see what happens if you send a little reminder to your heart that there's always a backstory. You don't have to know what the story is, but just remembering it's there can help you respond with compassion.

Exercise #3: Set an intention to view rude behavior as an opportunity.

Anytime someone is unkind, they are giving you an opportunity to stretch your kindness muscles. To help you embrace this opportunity, you might set an intention to view rude behavior as an opportunity this week. An *intention*, or a guiding principle for how you want to live, is a powerful way to change a habit—and how we respond to rude behavior is simply a habit we've adopted.

To set an intention, write an intention statement such as, *Today I will view any rude behavior as an opportunity for personal growth*, on a piece of paper or sticky note. Place your intention note somewhere you will see it regularly, such as on your bathroom mirror or computer screen. Then recite your intention first thing in the morning and again every time you see it.

Here are some intention statements to consider:

Today I will view any rude behavior as an opportunity to expand my interpersonal skills.

Today I will view any rude behavior as an opportunity for personal growth.

Today I will view any rude behavior as an opportunity to be kind.

Exercise #4: Write about it.

If you find yourself ruminating about something someone said or did this week, try writing about the incident. To do this, simply write down your deepest thoughts and emotions about what happened. If you feel like it will be helpful, consider writing about the incident for several days in a row.

CELESTE'S JOURNAL ENTRY: Kindness Neutralizes Road Rage

While I was driving to an appointment, a car cut dangerously in front of me. *What the hell!* I screamed in my mind. Feeling tense, upset, and angry, I sped up and tailgated the driver.

Then I remembered that I was practicing meeting rudeness with love this week. I knew I couldn't do this when I was angry, so I decided to try soothing myself with the "name it to tame it'" approach. I proclaimed aloud, "I am feeling really angry right now! My muscles are tense and I'm gripping the steering wheel tightly."—and to my amazement, it took so much bite out of my anger that I actually backed away from the driver.

What I had done was mostly a kindness to myself because the other driver probably didn't even know I was angry with him. And even if he had known—perhaps after I had tailgated him for miles—it was unlikely to make him a kinder driver. It would likely just piss him off. Why spread that around?

CHAPTER 12

Make Time

If we are too busy to be kind, we are too busy.
—Allan Lokos

It was a busy Sunday for Jesuit priest and author Father Gregory Boyle. After morning mass he rushed to his office to get through the day's mail before performing a baptism—but that's when Carmen, a gang member and heroin addict, entered his office. As she plopped down on his couch and launched into the heartbreaking story of her addiction, Father Boyle subtly kept his eye on the clock, inwardly lamenting that he probably wouldn't have any time that day to review the mail.

Midway through Carmen recounting her life story, Father Boyle observed her eyes pooling with tears. Then, after sharing how she had been trying to stop heroin ever since she started, Carmen looked directly at Boyle and haltingly declared, "I . . . am . . . a . . . disgrace."

As Father Boyle then recounted in his book *Tattoos on the Heart*, "Suddenly, her shame meets mine. For when Carmen walked through that door, I had mistaken her for an interruption."[103]

It's hard to be kind when we're stuck in the mantra of *I don't have enough time.* The results of a study led by Princeton social psychologists John Darley and Daniel Batson suggested that time pressure, or the psychological stress experienced when we worry about not having enough time, is a major roadblock to kindness.[104]

In the study, sixty-seven seminary students were told to go to another building to complete a task. The task the students were asked to do varied: one set of students was asked to give a talk on seminary jobs, while another set was asked to speak about the story of the Good Samaritan, a Bible story about helping strangers in need. The researchers also varied the time urgency for the students, telling some they were "late for the task," while telling others they had "plenty of time." Moreover, on the way to do their respective task, all the students passed by a man slumped in an alleyway who clearly needed assistance (the man was an actor planted by the researchers).

The researchers found that only 10 percent of the "late" students stopped to help the man even if they were the students who were going to speak on the parable of the Good Samaritan. Some of these "late" seminary students literally *stepped over* the man on the way to the next building! In stark comparison, 63 percent of the students who were told they had

"plenty of time" stopped to help the stranger in need.
Not only can we end up being less kind when pressured by time constraints, but time pressure is also unkind to us. It puts our mind into a worried state: we become worried about time or the lack thereof, worried about the number of things we have to do, and worried that we'll fail to achieve something important. All this worry can make us feel tense, stressed, edgy, and unhappy. And all this stress and worry is not good for our health, either!

To make matters worse, time pressure also hampers our productivity: when we are feeling pressured, we are in a state of stress, which narrows our ability to think clearly and function effectively. And research suggests that this actually makes us accomplish less.[105] Don't believe it? Well, have you ever gotten stumped by a problem, decided to take a break, and then later found that the answer magically came to you in a burst of inspiration? Or gone to sleep with a problem unsolved—and woken up the next morning with a clear answer? If so, then you've experienced how important a calm mind is for getting things done.

A final reason time pressure is unkind to us is that it may cause us to spend less time caring for ourselves just so we can "power through" and get more accomplished. Thus, we might do things like working through breaks, neglecting to take the time for nourishing meals, skipping that workout, or even cutting back on sleep. While doing so may seem like a helpful hack for dealing with stress and pressure, skimping on self-care backfires because our needs are necessary not only for our own happiness, but to simply function at our best and prevent even more stress, burnout, and sickness.

Top Time-Pressure Relievers

If we only felt time pressure once in a while, that wouldn't be so bad. The problem is that we live in a fast-paced, hurried world where most of us feel like we're in a constant battle with time. The good news is that it doesn't have to be this way. Louis and I want to share two simple and effective methods for taking the time pressure off so you can be healthier and happier, achieve more, and be kinder.

Time-pressure reliever #1: Create more time in your life

One way to take the pressure off is to find simple ways to create more time in your life. Here are some ways to achieve that:

- **Spend less time watching TV or on social media.** If you continue to watch a show you've grown tired of, can you let it go? And if you check the news or Facebook a bit less, you may gain a significant chunk of time each day.

- **Wake up half an hour earlier.** By getting up earlier, you can dedicate that extra time for meaningful activities like self-care, connecting with loved ones, stress management, or practicing kindness. However, please don't consider this option if it means you will not get adequate rest, as this is not kind to you.

- **Shop online.** Purchasing goods online is a fantastic time-saving opportunity. Instead of spending your valuable time traveling to stores, dragging through aisles, and waiting in line, you can shop online at the click of a mouse. In recent years, online food shopping has become particularly popular because it can save a huge amount of time. While an entire afternoon may need to be set aside for traditional grocery shopping, online shopping can be done in minutes. Working mother of three Maria shares that ordering groceries through Instacart and clothes through Stitch Fix has given her more precious time for what's most important.[106]

- **Simplify your life.** Living a simpler life means letting go of the less important so you can create more time for what's more important. Consider giving up those activities, magazine subscriptions, and relationships that are not supporting your well-being or values. You might even think about downsizing your home (think "tiny house") or material possessions to save time on organizing and cleaning.

- **Buy yourself some time.** If possible, spend less money buying stuff and more money buying time. How? Instead of a new dress, pair of jeans, or the latest and greatest electronic gadget, spend those dollars on time-saving services like house cleaning (yes, Louis and I are suggesting you get yourself that maid) or yard care. Or invest in time-saving devices such as a smart vacuum that cleans your floor or carpet by itself—no time on your part needed.

- **Say "yes" less often.** When cultivating kindness, saying "yes" is nuanced. Sometimes it is kinder to say "yes," and other times saying "no" is a kinder response. If a request will prevent you from having the time to care for yourself or your family, for example, then saying "no" may be a kinder choice.

Even when it's a kinder response, "no" can often be hard to say. A helpful hack I learned as a psychotherapy intern from my supervisor, Dr. Paul Foxman, is to say, "Let me think about it and get back to you," to every request. Then do just that.

Time-pressure reliever #2: Practice stress management

When you are feeling overwhelmed by the pressure of not having enough time, your body is in fight, flight, or freeze mode, where your sympathetic nervous system is pumping out stress hormones such as cortisol. Stress makes you unhappy, less kind, and less productive. To effectively combat stress, you need to switch to a parasympathetic mode, where your body produces feel-good chemicals, such as serotonin, that help you feel calm.

Here are some simple stress management methods that can take the pressure off.

- **Take regular restorative breaks.** By restorative, we mean doing something nonstriving, where you're not trying to accomplish anything except relaxing or having fun. Restorative things you can do include taking a walk, listening to your favorite tunes, socializing, doing something fun, being creative, or eating a healthy snack. My favorite things to do on a break are to chat with a friend, listen (and sometimes dance) to some favorite tunes, or go for a scenic walk in my neighborhood without my iPhone, making a point to notice as many pleasurable things as possible—the warm sun, a beautiful tree, an interesting building, the song of a bird, a smiling face.

- **Move your body.** Physical exercise is a great way to manage stress because it can improve your mood and help you relax. It can also improve your sleep, which is often disrupted by stress. Almost any form of movement can decrease your stress levels, so why not choose something you love? For Louis, it's running and yoga, whereas I'm a fan of cardio kickboxing, Ping-Pong, and dancing in the living room with my dog. Other examples include walking, swimming, playing tennis, and gardening.

- **Do an act of kindness.** We learned in chapter 3 that being kind might be an effective stress management practice. While it may feel like the last thing you want to do when you're stressed out, reaching out to help someone else will distract you from your own worries and issues and help you feel calm.

- **Laugh.** It's hard to feel stressed when we're laughing. This is because it relieves tension by relaxing our muscles and triggering the release of endorphins, which promote an overall sense of well-being. One study found that participants who did a "laughter intervention" experienced more stress relief than those who were simply distracted.[107]

So, try watching a comedy movie, going to an

improv show, hanging out with friends who make you laugh, or taking a Laughter Yoga class. Laughter Yoga is exercises designed to get people to laugh for no reason combined with simple yoga breathing techniques (classes are typically free).

- **Slow down.** Many of us react to time pressure by rushing, which backfires. Instead of helping us accomplish more, this fuels our stress. A more helpful response is to intentionally slow down, which signals our body that there is no danger and allows us to relax. As the body calms, we're able to think more clearly, function more effectively, and accomplish more. Psychologist and Buddhist meditation teacher Tara Brach suggests saying to yourself, *There's no need to rush,* whenever you notice you're feeling pressured.[108] Not as an authoritarian demand, but more as an invitation to just slow down.

- **Socialize.** Spending time with friends and family is so important for emotional well-being that my sister and I have dubbed it "vitamin S." Whenever one of us is stressed out, we ask the other, "Did you get your vitamin S today?"

  While socializing is beneficial for everyone, one study found that for women in particular, it helps release oxytocin, a natural stress reliever.[109] You might have lunch with a coworker, call a friend, FaceTime with a parent or child, or go for a walk with a neighbor.

- **Set aside one day a week for rest.** "One of the reasons many of us keep busy schedules is we fail to recognize the value of rest," says Joshua Becker on his Becoming Minimalist blog. "But rest is beneficial to our bodies, our minds, and our souls. Set aside one day per week for rest and family. Intentionally schedule it on your calendar. Then, guard it at all costs."[110]

- **Meditate.** Feeling busy comes from thinking about the future and not being in the moment. It fuels our stress response to worry about the future. Meditation calms the mind because it gives your mind just one thing to do. In a nutshell, meditation means paying attention to just one thing, such as your breath, a candle flame, or even the coffee you're sipping. Since there are a variety of things you can pay attention to, meditation can look like a lot of different things depending on what works for you.

  You may want to start with a breath meditation because it's simple to learn (see the following directions). Or if that doesn't appeal to you, explore Insight Timer, a free meditation app that has hundreds of meditations you can try.

  It is important to note that while meditation may help you deal with stress in the short term, it is generally not a quick fix. I once saw a cartoon caption of a woman sitting in a Lotus meditation pose with the caption: "Come on . . . come ON . . . inner peace . . . I don't have all day!" It doesn't work that way. Instead, the practice trains your brain over time to experience greater well-being and peace.

Three-Minute Breath Meditation

Try this simple, three-minute meditation:

- **Get in a comfortable sitting or lying position and set a timer for three minutes.** Let your eyes gently close.
- **Focus on your breath.** Now simply begin focusing your attention on your breathing. Where do you feel your breath most? The rising and falling in your belly? The air as it enters and exits your nostrils? Try to keep your focus on your inhale and exhale.
- **Keep bringing your focus back to your breath.** Whenever you notice your mind wandering, gently bring your attention back to your breath. Don't worry if your mind wanders a lot; this is normal. Simply continue bringing your attention back to your breath until your alarm goes off.

Exercises

Exercise #1: Log how you spend your time.

To know how to create more time in your life, you first need to know exactly how you're spending it. You say you don't have enough time to do everything on your to-do list, let alone to practice kindness, but why not find out for sure?

Try keeping a log of how you spend your time this week. You can do this in a notebook or use a spreadsheet or time-tracking app—whatever works. When you actually track your time, you'll likely discover some pockets of time you can redeploy for meaningful activities.

Exercise #2: Create more time in your life this week.

There are literally hundreds of ways to create more time in your life. The method or methods that will work for you will be unique to your personality and lifestyle. To find a helpful method for you, review the methods listed in this chapter, or try the sentence completion technique developed by psychotherapist Nathaniel Branden, which often helps people come up with insights that bring about meaningful change in their lives.

To do the sentence completion technique, write down the sentence stem *An effective way to create more time in my life might be* . . . and then quickly write at least six endings or as many as you can think of. After you generate your responses, go over them and see if you wish to act on any of the ideas. If not, repeat the exercise again. It may take a few trials to find something you want to do.

Here is an example of the sentence stem completed with six endings:

An effective way to create more time in my life might be . . .

. . . to stop hitting the snooze button on my alarm clock.

. . . to say "no" to everything except essential requests.

. . . to let go of having a perfectly clean house.

. . . to do my workouts at home instead of going to the gym.

. . . to watch TV for half an hour less than I usually do every day.

. . . to buy precut veggies and prepared foods.

Exercise #3: Try a stress management method.

Choose a stress management activity such as the ones listed in this chapter or another method of your choice, and make a point to try it this week.

Exercise #4: Make time to be kind to you!

You'd likely encourage a busy or stressed-out friend to make time to take care of herself, but do you give this kindness to yourself? Self-care is not selfish! Many of us have been programmed to think we have to put the needs of everyone else first, but can you give of yourself authentically when you're running on empty? If you give from a place of empty, you're just giving from a place of anxiety and tension, and people around you sense that.

But when you take good care of yourself, you not only feel peace, but you share that with everyone around you.

Self-care, which means taking an active role in promoting and maintaining your well-being, is not one size fits all. For me, it starts with exercising first thing in the morning, meditating and/or praying for twenty minutes, eating healthfully, taking regular breaks, and finding ways to smile, laugh, and connect every day. Some days it seems impossible to do. Other days I succeed and feel so much better and wonder why I ever neglect my basic needs. Make it a priority this week to practice self-care in a way that feels right and feasible for you.

CELESTE'S JOURNAL ENTRY: A Lesson in Kindness from My Dog

I normally take my adorable fluffy white dog, Mambo, to a local trail where he can run in the morning. He's a high-energy dog, so he really needs this. However, one day I was feeling pressure to make progress on the book I was collaborating on with a colleague (this book!), so I just walked him around the block. This came back to "bite me."

As soon as I sat down to write, Mambo dropped a toy on my lap, urging me to play with him. "Sorry, Mambo, I'm busy," I said as I dropped the toy on the floor. He immediately picked it up and dropped it on my lap again. I left the toy on my lap and ignored him.

Mambo snagged the toy and began playing with it on his

own. He squeaked it over and over again, annoying me, so I took the toy away from him. He hadn't given up, however. He sat right next to me, making focused eye contact and grunting to get my attention. His anxious energy bothered me, so I told him to "go lie down." He didn't move. After a moment or two of this, he bumped his nose against my leg to get my attention. I told him to go lie down more sternly—which worked, but after a few minutes, he was back again.

After another fifteen minutes of Mambo's antics, I was fuming and shouted at him. Then I picked him up, put him out of the room, and slammed the door. I felt bad for doing this, but what I was working on was important. I was writing a book on kindness, and it was going to make a difference in people's lives. I hadn't been able to work on it for a while, and I really felt pressure to make progress on it.

I wrote undisturbed for about half an hour and then took a break to get something to drink. As I walked into the kitchen, I saw Mambo sitting in the middle of the room quaking with fear. My heart sank. Horrified that I had frightened my beloved dog like that, I rushed over to him and picked him up. I held him in a tight hug for a long time until he stopped shaking.

This incident hit me hard. The time pressure I was putting on myself to complete the kindness book was preventing me from being kind. Apparently *I* was the one who needed a lesson in kindness. After thinking deeply about this, I decided to hire a dog walker twice a week. This has really eased my stress, and it's made Mambo happier too.

Epilogue

In the end, only kindness matters.
—Jewel

May you awaken to your power. Your own happiness and the world's happiness begin with you! One of the most powerful ways you can create this change is through kindness: kindness in your thoughts and actions toward yourself and every sentient being you think about or encounter each day. By taking one small step for kindness today, you are taking one giant leap for the happiness of the world.

Acknowledgments

I have to start by thanking my awesome collaborator, Louis. From believing in me when this book was just an idea to encouraging me throughout the long learning curve to providing additions and edits that helped maintain this book's evidence-based standard, his contributions meant more than I think even he realizes.

I know that this book never would have been completed without the love, patience, and support of my husband, Paul. He was the one who had to field daily "What do you think of this paragraph?" questions, lift my spirits when I wanted to give up, and continue to love me despite how annoying I was throughout the writing process.

My parents, Ron and Lorrie, have continuously supported my writing since I was in the fifth grade and told them I liked creative writing. This has meant more than they know. I also wish to thank them deeply for being outstanding role models of kindness.

I have been blessed to have immense encouragement and help on this project from my siblings, in-laws, and extended family. While I'm so thankful to all of them, several of them went above and beyond. Michelle, I appreciate your gigantic belief in me, ongoing encouragement, and sincere excitement about this book. Lee, you gave me confidence that this book was worthwhile because you read an early copy of this manuscript simply because you wanted to, not because I asked you to. Mark and Maria, you guys have made me feel like my writing must be enjoyable because you regularly read my previous blog. Rose, you have been an ongoing support for me throughout this project, and I really appreciate that! John, I appreciate that you recently told me my master's thesis was "really good." This boosted my confidence in my writing ability.

There are so many friends who have helped me bring this book into the world. I want to give a special shout-out to Shannon, Diana, Anna, Pat, Sid, Susan, Mary, and Carla for their ongoing belief and support with my writing and with this book. Thank you all so much!

I would also like to thank Paul Foxman for supporting and encouraging me in my writing over the past ten years. It means so much to me that he's taken time out of his busy schedule to read and provide feedback on parts of this and other writing projects.

It was helpful to process an early draft of this manuscript through the Theano Coaching & Writers' Workshops. I want to give a heartfelt thank-you to Kathryn Britton, Jan Stanley, and Kim Wimmer for their thoughts, ideas, and support. And an extra gigantic thank-you to Jan and Kim for reading and sharing their thoughts on the completed manuscript. This was a kindness that I am exceptionally grateful for.

I also wish to thank Stephanie, who read through the first draft and offered me invaluable feedback and insights that greatly enhanced the book. Her efforts are much appreciated!

Another person I wish to thank is Jeanne Sanner for reading and sharing her thoughts on parts of this book. Her books and spiritual lessons have also inspired parts of this book. I am very grateful for her support and wise counsel.

I'd like to express a big thank-you to all my relatives, friends, neighbors, and acquaintances who provided stories for this book. You have really helped me bring this book to life!

I wish to express my heartfelt gratitude to Elizabeth Zack and Christina Roth for skillfully editing this book. When I read Elizabeth's sample edit, I knew she was the perfect developmental editor for this book. And I was right! She not only highlighted issues that needed to be addressed but also helped make this book a joy to read. Then Christina's thoroughness, attention to detail, and fact-checking as this book's copyeditor impressed me and made me feel ready to share this book with the world.

Huge big thanks to Asya Blue, who did the cover design and book design. Not only were her talent and artistry top notch, but she was also patient, understanding, and lovely to work with!

Thank you also to Reedsy, the online author services company that made it easy for me to find the skillful designer and editors who took this book to the next level.

And last but certainly not least, I want to thank God for the numerous bursts of inspiration that I'm 89 percent convinced came from above.

About the Authors

CELESTE DIMILLA, MS, LMFT, CAPP is a licensed psychotherapist and author. She teaches and writes about simple practices that help people to be their happiest and most loving selves. She believes that greater happiness is possible for everyone, and it's simple once you learn what really works to boost happiness. She lives in Orange County, California, with her husband, Paul, and fluffy white dog, Mambo.

LOUIS ALLORO, MEd, MAPP is a positive psychology scholar practitioner who designs and delivers highly sought-after, evidence-based well-being and positive change learning experiences around the world. A senior fellow at the Center for the Advancement of Well-Being, cofounder of the Change Lab, a Michelle McQuaid initiative, and co-creator of the new Certificate in Creating Wellbeing, a one-hundred-hour training program for companies, campuses, and cities to empower and rally internal change champions to be the change they wish to see, he is currently pursuing his PhD in systems informed positive psychology and social impact evaluation.

NOTES AND REFERENCES

Introduction

[1] Miller, C. A., & Frisch, M. B. (2011). *Creating your best life: The ultimate list guide*. Sterling.

[2] Zimmer, E. (Host). (2016, May 14). The #1 mistake people make when trying to change behavior (No. unknown) [Audio podcast episode]. In *The one you feed*. The one you feed. https://art19.com/shows/the-one-you-feed/episodes/aff77940-2b0e-43f9-bf2f-783580431106

Chapter 1: A Fresh Look at Kindness

[3] Forrest, M. S. (2003). *A short course in kindness: A little book on the importance of love and the relative unimportance of just about everything else*. L. M. Press.

[4] Salzberg, S. (2002). *Lovingkindness: The revolutionary art of happiness*. Shambhala.

[5] Chodron, P. (2007). *Practicing peace in times of war*. Shambhala.

[6] Gibran, K. (2013). *The treasured writings of Kahlil Gibran: Author of the prophet*. Castle Books.

[7] Ricard, M. (2016). *A plea for the animals: The moral, philosophical, and evolutionary imperative to treat all beings with compassion*. Shambhala.

Chapter 2: Why Being Kind Makes *You* (Not Just Others) Happy

[8] Lyubomirsky, S. (2007). *The how of happiness: A new approach to getting the life you want*. Penguin Books.

[9] Curry, O., Rowland, L. A., VanLissa, C. J., Zlotowitz, S., McAlaney, J., & Whitehouse, H. (2018). Happy to help? A systematic review and meta-analysis of the effects of performing acts of kindness on the well-being of the actor. *Journal of Experimental Social Psychology, 76*, 320–329.

[10] Rowland, L., & Curry, O. (2019). A range of kindness activities boost happiness. *Journal of Social Psychology, 159*(3), 340–343.

[11] Buchanan, K., & Bardi, A. (2010). Acts of kindness and acts of novelty affect life satisfaction. *Journal of Social Psychology, 150*(3), 235–237.

[12] Steger, M., Kashdan, T., & Oishi, S. (2008). Being good by doing good: Daily eudaimonic activity and well-being. *Journal of Research in Personality, 42*(1), 22–42.

[13] Dunn, E. W., Aknin, L. B., & Norton, M. I. (2008). Spending money on others promotes happiness. *Science, 319*(5870), 1687–1688.

[14] Harbaugh, W. T., Mayr, U., & Burghart, D. R. (2007). Neural responses to taxation and voluntary giving reveal motives for charitable donations. *Science, 316* (5831), 1622–1625.

[15] Zhivotovskaya, E. (2014). *Certificate in applied positive psychology manual: A scientific guide to flourishing* [Unpublished Manuscript].

[16] Lyubomirsky, S. (2007). *The how of happiness: A new approach to getting the life you want.* Penguin Books.

[17] Trivers, R. (1971). The evolution of reciprocal altruism. *Quarterly Review of Biology, 46*(1), 35–57.

[18] Smith, C., & Davidson, H. (2014). *The paradox of generosity: Giving we receive, grasping we lose.* Oxford University Press.

[19] Krause, N., Herzog, A. R., & Baker, E. (1992). Providing support to others and well-being in later life. *Journal of Gerontology, 47*(5), 300–311.

[20] Hunter, K., & Linn, M. (1980–81). Psychosocial differences between elderly volunteers and non-volunteers. *International Journal of Aging and Human Development, 12*(3), 205–213.

[21] Musick, M. A., & Wilson, J. (2003). Volunteering and depression: The role of psychological and social resources in different age groups. *Social Science and Medicine, 56*(2), 259–269.

[22] Hamilton, D. R. (2017). *The five side effects of kindness: This book will make you feel better, be happier & live longer.* Hay House UK.

[23] Random Acts of Kindness Foundation. (2019, October 21). *The world needs more love letters* [Video]. YouTube. youtube.com/watch?v=VopcuymgUCA

Chapter 3: The Benefits of Kindness

[24] Keyes, C. L. M., & Haidt, J. (2003). *Flourishing: Positive psychology and the life well-lived.* APA Books.

[25] Schnall, S., Roper, J., & Fessler, D. M. (2010). Elevation leads to altruistic behavior. *Psychological Science, 21*(3), 315–320.

[26] Fowler, J., & Christakis, N. (2010). Cooperative behavior cascades in human social networks. *PNAS, 107*(12), 5334–5338.

[27] Life Vest Inside. (2011, August 29). *Kindness boomerang – "one day"* [Video]. YouTube. youtube.com/watch?v=nwAYpLVyeFU

[28] Mayo Clinic. (2019, April 4). *Healthy lifestyle: Stress management.* mayoclinic .org/healthy-lifestyle/stress-management/basics/stress-basics/hlv-20049495

[29] Mental Health Foundation. (2018, May). *Stress: Are we coping?* London: Mental Health Foundation. https://www.mentalhealth.org.uk/publications/stress-are -we-coping

[30] Raposa, E. B., Laws, H. B., & Ansell, E. B. (2016). Prosocial behavior mitigates the negative effects of stress in everyday life. *Clinical Psychological Science, 4*(4), 691–698.

[31] Luks, A., & Payne, P. (1992). *The healing power of doing good: The health and spiritual benefits of helping others.* iUniverse.com, Inc.

[32] Dignity Health Study. (2019, September). *Study shows giving and receiving kindness during holiday travel relieves stress.* Dignity Health. https:// www.dignityhealth.org/central-california/about-us/hello-healthy/hello-healthy -articles/study-shows-giving-and-receiving-kindness-during-holiday-travel -relieves-stress

[33] Dignity Health Study. (2019, September). *Study shows giving and receiving kindness during holiday travel relieves stress.* Dignity Health. https:// www.dignityhealth.org/central-california/about-us/hello-healthy/hello-healthy -articles/study-shows-giving-and-receiving-kindness-during-holiday-travel -relieves-stress

[34] Homan, K. S., & Sirois, F. M. (2017). Self-compassion and physical health: Exploring the roles of perceived stress and health-promoting behaviors. *Health Psychology Open, 4*(2), 1–9.

[35] Luks, A., & Payne, P. (1992). *The healing power of doing good: The health and spiritual benefits of helping others.* iUniverse.com, Inc.

[36] Hamilton, D. R. (2017). *The five side effects of kindness: This book will make you feel better, be happier & live longer.* Hay House UK.

[37] Arnstein, P., Vidal, M., Wells-Federman, C., Morgan, B., & Caudill, M. (2002). From chronic pain patient to peer: Benefits and risks of volunteering. *Pain Management in Nursing, 3*(3), 94–103.

[38] Hamilton, D. R. (2010). *Why kindness is good for you.* Hay House UK.

[39] Nerem, R. M., Levesque, M. J., & Cornhill, J. F. (1980). Social environment as a factor in diet-induced atherosclerosis. *Science, 208*(4451), 1475–1476.

[40] Felps, P. (Host). (2019, August 20). Living longer and happier through kindness with Kelli Harding (Season 5 No. 3) [Audio podcast episode]. In *Live happy now.* Live Happy Now.

[41] Spitz R., & Wolf K. (1946). Anaclitic depression: An inquiry into the genesis of psychiatric conditions in early childhood II. *The Psychoanalytic Study of the Child, 2*(1), 313–342.

[42] Cohen S., Janicki-Deverts, D., Turner, R. B., & Doyle, W. J. (2015). Does hugging provide stress-buffering social support? A study of susceptibility to upper respiratory infection and illness. *Psychological Science, 26*(2), 135–147.

[43] Harding, K. (2019). *The rabbit effect: Live longer, happier, and healthier with the groundbreaking science of kindness.* Atria Books.

[44] Thomas, A. G., Jonason, P. K., Blackburn, J. D., Kennair, L. O., Lowe, R., Malouff, J., Stewart-Williams, S., Sulikowski, D., & Li, N. P. (2019). Mate preference priorities in the East and West: A cross-cultural test of the mate preference priority model. *Journal of Personality*, 1–15.

[45] Zhang, Y., Kong, F., & Kou, H. (2014). Personality manipulations: Do they modulate facial attractiveness ratings? *Personality and Individual Differences, 70*, 80–84.

[46] Chopik, W., & Lucas, R. E. (2019). Actor, partner, and similarity effects of personality on global and experienced well-being. *Journal of Research in Personality, 78*, 249–261.

[47] Gottman, J. M. (1993). *What predicts divorce? The relationship between marital processes and marital outcomes.* Psychology Press.

[48] Layous, K., Nelson, K. S., Oberle, E., Schonert-Reichl, K. A., & Lyubomirsky, S. (2012). *Kindness counts: Prompting prosocial behavior in preadolescents boosts peer acceptance and well-being.* https://doi.org/10.1371/journal.pone.0051380

Chapter 4: Just *Why* You Are Going to Succeed

[49] S. Brown (personal communication, November 4, 2020).

[50] Babauta, L. (2013, February 13). The four habits that form habits. *Zen Habits.* zenhabits.net/habitses/#:~:text=By%20Leo%20Babauta&text=The%20solution%20is%20exceedingly%20simple,to%20do%20more%20than%20that

[51] McQuaid, M. (Host). (2018, March 22). Do you need a play mindset? (No. 89) [Audio podcast episode]. In *Making positive psychology work.* Michelle McQuaid. michellemcquaid.com/podcast/need-play-mindset-podcast-stella-grizont/

[52] Fields, R. (2013). *A year of living with more compassion: 52 quotes & weekly compassion practices.* FACES Publishing.

[53] Poehler, A. (2011, May 26). *Harvard university 2011 class day speech by Amy Poehler* [Speech audio recording]. YouTube. youtube.com/watch?v=7WvdxgGpNVU

[54] Chopra, D. (2005). Cover endorsement. In S. Grayson, *Journalution: Journaling to awaken your inner voice, heal your life, and manifest your dreams.* New World Library.

Chapter 5: Find a Friend in You

[55] Phillips, N. (Host). (2018, March 8). *Lisa Williams* (No. 22) [Audio podcast episode]. In *The kindness podcast*. NPR. npr.org/podcasts/557154160/the -kindness-podcast

[56] Neff, K. (2015). *Self-compassion: The proven power of being kind to yourself.* William Morrow Paperbacks.

[57] Research studies on self-criticism are summarized in clinical health psychologist and interdisciplinary stress/psychology researcher Golan Shahar's book *Erosion: The psychopathology of self-criticism.* (2015) Oxford University Press.

[58] Neff, K. (Date unknown). *Why we need to have compassion for our inner critic.* self-compassion.org. https://self-compassion.org/why-we-need-to-have-compassion-for-our-inner-critic/#:~:text=Our%20inner%20critic%20wants%20us,way%20to%20go%20about%20it.&text=And%20believe%20it%20or%20not,into%20our%20other%20safety%20system

[59] For example, see: Breines, J. G., & Chen, S. (2012). Self-compassion increases self-improvement motivation. *Personality and Social Psychology Bulletin, 38*(9), 1133–1143. And Adams, C. E., & Leary, M. R. (2007). Promoting self -compassionate attitudes toward eating among restrictive and guilty eaters. *Journal of Social and Clinical Psychology, 26*(10), 1120–1144.

[60] Yazdi, P. (2020, January 5). *9 beneficial effects of oxytocin + 34 ways to increase it.* Self Hacked. selfhacked.com/blog/the-social-chilled-out-and-empathetic-genes -oxytocin-receptor-snps/

[61] Neff, K. (2020). *Self-Compassion Publications.* Self-Compassion. https://self -compassion.org/the-research/

[62] Neff, K. D., Rude, S. S., & Kirkpatrick, K. L. (2007). An examination of self-compassion in relation to positive psychological functioning and personality traits. *Journal of Research in Personality, 41*(4), 908–916.

[63] Neff, K. D., & Vonk, R. (2008). Self-compassion versus global self-esteem: Two different ways of relating to oneself. *Journal of Personality, 77*, 23–50. https://doi.org/10.1111/j.1467-6494.2008.00537.x

[64] Adams, C. E., & Leary, M. R. (2007). Promoting self-compassionate attitudes toward eating among restrictive and guilty eaters. *Journal of Social and Clinical Psychology, 26*(10), 1120–1144.

[65] Breines, J. G., & Chen, S. (2012). Self-compassion increases self-improvement motivation. *Personality and Social Psychology Bulletin, 38*(9), 1133–1143.

[66] Brown, B. (2013, January 14). *Shame v. guilt.* brenebrown.com. brenebrown.com/blog/2013/01/14/shame-v-guilt/

[67] Brown, B. (2015). *Daring greatly: How the courage to be vulnerable transforms the way we live, love, parent, and lead.* Avery.

[68] Hay, L. L. (1995). *You can heal your life.* Hay House Inc.

Chapter 6: Create "Micro-Moments" of Love

[69] Fredrickson, B. L. (2013). *Love 2.0: Creating happiness and health in moments of connection.* Plume.

[70] Fredrickson, B. L. (Date unknown). What is love? *Farnam Street.* fs.blog/2014/02/barbara-fredrickson-love/

[71] Sandstrom, G. M., & Dunn, E. W. (2014). Is efficiency overrated? Minimal social interactions lead to belonging and positive affect. *Social Psychological and Personality Science, 5*(4), 437–442.

[72] Lyubomirsky, S. (2007). *The how of happiness: A new approach to getting the life you want.* Penguin Books.

Chapter 7: Step Up Your Generosity

[73] Smith, C., & Davidson, H. (2014). *The paradox of generosity: Giving we receive, grasping we lose.* Oxford University Press.

[74] Dunn, E. W., Akin, L. B., & Norton, M. I. (2008). Spending money on others promotes happiness. *Science, 319*(5870), 1687–1688.

[75] Salzberg, S. (2002). *Lovingkindness: The revolutionary art of happiness.* Shambhala.

Chapter 8: Practice Loving-Kindness

[76] Gentile, D. A., Sweet, D. M., & He, L. (2020). Caring for others cares for the self: An experimental test of brief downward social comparison, loving-kindness, and interconnectedness contemplations. *Journal of Happiness Studies, 21*, 765–778.

[77] Fredrickson, B. L., Cohn, M. A., Coffey, K. A., Pek, J., & Finkel, S. M. (2008). Open hearts build lives: Positive emotions, induced through loving-kindness meditation, build consequential personal resources. *Journal of Personality and Social Psychology, 95*(5), 1045–1062.

[78] Kearney, D. J., Malte, C. A., McManus, C., Martinez, M. E., Fellerman, B., & Simpson, T. L. (2013). Loving-kindness meditation for posttraumatic stress disorder: A pilot study. *Journal of Traumatic Stress, 26*(4), 426–434.

[79] Tonelli, M. E., & Wachholtz, A. B. (2014). Meditation-based treatment yielding immediate relief for meditation-naïve migraineurs. *Pain Management Nursing, 15*(1), 36–40.

[80] Carson, J. W., Keefe, F. J., Lynch, T. R., Carson, K. M., Goli, V., Fras, A. M., & Thorp, S. R. (2005). Loving-kindness meditation for chronic low back pain: Results from a pilot trial. *Journal of Holistic Nursing, 23*(3), 287–304.

[81] Kang, Y., Gray, J. R., & Dovidio, J. F. (2014). The nondiscriminating heart: Lovingkindness meditation training decreases implicit intergroup bias. *Journal of Experimental Psychology: General, 143*(3), 1306–1313.

[82] Shahar, B., Szsepsenwol, O., Zilcha-Mano, S., Haim, N., Zamir, O., Levi -Yeshuvi, S., & Levit-Binnun, N. A. (2015). A wait-list randomized controlled trial of loving-kindness meditation programme for self-criticism. *Clinical Psychology & Psychotherapy, 22*(4), 346–356.

Chapter 9: Open Your Heart to Suffering

[83] Worline, M. C., & Dutton, J. E. (2017). *Awakening compassion at work: The quiet power that elevates people and organizations.* Berrett-Koehler.

[84] Singer, T., & Klimecki, O. M. (2014). Empathy and compassion. *Current Biology, 24*(18), 875–878.

[85] Harling, B. (2017). *How to listen so people will talk: Build stronger communication and deeper connections.* Bethany House.

[86] Harling, B. (2017). *How to listen so people will talk: Build stronger communication and deeper connections.* Bethany House.

Chapter 10: Do Random Acts of Kindness

[87] Pressman, S. D., Kraft, T. L., & Cross, M. P. (2015). It's good to do good and receive good: The impact of a 'pay it forward' style kindness intervention on giver and receiver well-being. *Journal of Positive Psychology, 10*(4), 293–302.

[88] Seligman, M. E. P. (2012). *Flourish: A visionary new understanding of happiness and well-being.* Atria Books.

[89] Seligman, M. E. P. (2012). *Flourish: A visionary new understanding of happiness and well-being.* Atria Books.

[90] Wahba, Orly. (2017). *Kindness boomerang: How to save the world (and yourself) through 365 daily acts.* Flatiron Books.

Chapter 11: Meet Rudeness with Love

[91] Salzberg, S. (2002). *Lovingkindness: The revolutionary art of happiness.* Shambhala.

[92] Porath, C. (2016). *Mastering civility: A manifesto for the workplace.* Grand Central Publishing.

[93] Robertson, K., & O'Reilly, J. (2019). "Killing them with kindness"? A study of service employees' responses to uncivil customers. *Journal of Organizational Behavior, 41*(8), 797–813.

[94] Robertson, K., & O'Reilly, J. (2019). "Killing them with kindness"? A study of service employees' responses to uncivil customers. *Journal of Organizational Behavior, 41*(8), 797–813.

[95] Foulk, T., Woolum, A., & Erez, A. (2016). Catching rudeness is like catching a cold: The contagious effects of low-intensity negative behaviors. *Journal of Applied Psychology, 101*(1), 50–67.

[96] Porath, C. L. (2016). *Mastering civility: A manifesto for the workplace.* Grand Central Publishing.

[97] Porath, C. L., & Erez, A. (2009). Overlooked but not untouched: How rudeness reduces onlookers' performance on routine and creative tasks. *Organizational Behavior and Human Decision Processes, 109*(1), 29–44.

[98] Porath, C. (2018, January). *Why being respectful to your coworkers is good for business* [Video]. TED Conferences. ted.com/talks/Christine_porath_why_being _respectful_to_your_coworkers_is_good_for_business?language=en

[99] Kircanski, K., Lieberman, M. D., & Craske, M. G. (2012). Feelings into words: Contributions of language to exposure therapy. *Psychological Science, 23*(10), 1086–1091.

[100] Sanner, J. (personal communication, January 20, 2021).

[101] Fredrickson, Barbara. (2009). *Positivity: Top-notch research reveals the 3-to-1 ratio that will change your life.* Harmony Books.

[102] Baikie, K. A., & Wilhelm, K. (2005). Emotional and physical health benefits of expressive writing. *Advances in Psychiatric Treatment, 11*(5), 338–346.

Chapter 12: Make Time

[103] DeDonno, M. A., & Demaree, H. A. (2008). Perception of time pressure impairs performance. *Judgment and Decision Making, 3*(1), 636–640.

[104] Darley, J. M., & Batson, C. D. (1973). "From Jerusalem to Jericho": A study of situational and dispositional variables in helping behavior. *Journal of Personality and Social Psychology, 27*(1), 100–106.

[105] DeDonno, M. A., & Demaree, H. A. (2008). Perception of time pressure impairs performance. *Judgment and Decision Making, 3*(1), 636–640.

[106] Wenzler, M. (personal communication, March 6, 2020).

[107] Bennett, M. P., Zeller, J. M., Rosenberg, L., & McCann, J. (2003). The effect of mirthful laughter on stress and natural killer cell activity. *Alternative Therapies in Health and Medicine, 9*(2), 38–45.

[108] Brach, T. (2017, April 26) Relaxing the over controller – Part 1. *Tara Brach.* tarabrach.com/relaxing-over-controller/

[109] Taylor, S. E., Klein, L. C., Lewis, B. P., Gruenewald, T. L., Gurung, R. A., & Updegraff, J. A. (2000). Biobehavioral responses to stress in females: Tend-and -befriend, not fight-or-flight. *Psychological Review, 107*(3), 411–429.

[110] Becker, J. (Date unknown). A helpful guide to becoming unbusy. *Becoming Minimalist.* becomingminimalist.com/un-busy/comment-page-3/

Made in the USA
Middletown, DE
03 March 2022

62065739R00109